1938

Toll House
Chocolate Crunch
Cookie makes its first
appearance in print in
the 1938 edition of *Ruth
Wakefield's Toll House
Tried and True Recipes.*

Researchers in Nestlé's
U.S. laboratories
create the first
imperishable coffee.
This innovative
product—the world's
first instant coffee—
makes its way to
the United States
as Nescafé® the
following year.

1939

Gerber introduces its
first baby cereal.

1947

Ruth Wakefield sells
Nestlé the right to use
her cookie recipe and
the Toll House name …
for $1.

1951

Dr. Lewis J. Minor, a
food scientist, founds
the L. J. Minor
Company in Cleveland,
Ohio, with $6,000 and
a borrowed mixer.
Dr. Minor hires chefs
to sell his product,
enforcing the
company's idea that the
product was created
by chefs, for chefs.

1957

Ralson Purina becomes
the first company to
use a manufacturing
process called
extrusion to make
dry dog food pieces
that are uniform in
size and appearance.

1965

Carnation® Instant
Breakfast is introduced

1974

OPTIFAST®, a
pioneering product
in medical weight
management,
is introduced.

Nestlé in the United States | 1866–1976

1938

Nestlé Crunch®
launched.

1943

Nestlé opens two
American production
facilities to keep up
with the growing
demand for Nescafé®.
The military supplies
the popular instant
coffee to US troops
during World War II.

1948

Nestlé launches Quik
Chocolate Powder,
allowing parents
all over the United
States to make their
children a quick glass
of chocolate milk.

Nestlé debuts its
Nestea® brand, so
consumers can make
iced tea by stirring
Nestea® crystals
into cold water.

1956

Friskies® canned cat
food is introduced by
Carnation Company.

1962

Purina Cat Chow®
debuts and quickly
becomes the country's
best-selling dry
cat food.

Tombstone® Pizza is
started by Wisconsin
bar owner Joe Simek.

1973

Stouffer's® joins the
Nestlé family
and launches its
popular frozen
French bread pizza the
following year.

1976

Nestlé purchases
Libby's®, the world's
premier canned
pumpkin producer.

NESTLÉ IN THE UNITED STATES

A CELEBRATION OF GOOD FOOD, GOOD LIFE

NESTLÉ IN THE UNITED STATES

A CELEBRATION OF GOOD FOOD, GOOD LIFE

JEFFREY L. RODENGEN

Introduction by
PAUL GRIMWOOD
Chairman and CEO, Nestlé USA

Edited by Kim Campbell
Design and layout by Darcey McNiff Thompson

Nestlé USA, Inc. and the publisher have made every effort to identify and locate the source of the photographs included in this edition of *Nestlé in the United States: A Celebration of Good Food, Good Life*. Grateful acknowledgment is made to those who have kindly granted permission for the use of their materials in this edition. If there are instances where proper credit was not given, we will gladly make any necessary corrections in subsequent printings.

All historical photographs appearing in the book are the property of Nestlé S.A./ Nestlé Historical Archives and/or Nestlé USA, Inc. and its affiliates, unless stated otherwise.

Also by Jeffrey L. Rodengen

The Legend of Chris-Craft

IRON FIST:
The Lives of Carl Kiekhaefer

Evinrude-Johnson
and The Legend of OMC

The Legend of
Dr Pepper/Seven-Up

The Legend of Honeywell

The Legend of Briggs & Stratton

The Legend of Ingersoll-Rand

The Legend of Stanley:
150 Years of The Stanley Works

The Legend of Halliburton

The Legend of Nucor Corporation

The Legend of Goodyear:
The First 100 Years

The Legend of Cessna

The Legend of VF Corporation

New Horizons:
The Story of Ashland Inc.

The History of American Standard

The Legend of Mercury Marine

The Legend of Pfizer

State of the Heart:
The Practical Guide to Your Heart
and Heart Surgery
WITH LARRY W. STEPHENSON, M.D.

The Legend of
Worthington Industries

The Legend of
Cornelius Vanderbilt Whitney

The Legend of Gulfstream

The Legend of Bertram
WITH DAVID A. PATTEN

The Ship in the Balloon:
The Story of Boston Scientific
and the Development of
Less-Invasive Medicine

NRA: An American Legend

The Legend of Grainger

The Legend of Polaris
WITH RICHARD F. HUBBARD

The Legend of La-Z-Boy
WITH RICHARD F. HUBBARD

Jefferson-Pilot Financial:
A Century of Excellence
WITH RICHARD F. HUBBARD

The Legend of HCA

The Legend of Sovereign Bancorp
WITH RICHARD F. HUBBARD

Changing the World:
Polytechnic University—
The First 150 Years

Cerner: From Vision to Value

Office Depot: Taking Care of
Business—The First 20 Years

Amica: A Century of Service
1907–2007

A Passion for Service:
The Story of ARAMARK

The Legend of Con-way:
A History of Service, Reliability,
Innovation, and Growth

Commanding the Waterways:
The Story of Sea Ray

Past, Present & Futures:
Chicago Mercantile Exchange

The Legend of Brink's

Kiewit: An Uncommon Company:
Celebrating the First 125 Years

Parker Hannifin Corporation:
A Winning Heritage

Innovation, Passion, Success:
The EMC Story

Powering Business:
100 Years of Eaton Corporation

Old Dominion Freight Line:
Helping the World Keep Promises

Improving the Human Condition:
The Story of Sanford Health

The Past is Prologue: The American
College of Cardiology — 65 Years
of Cardiovascular Innovation

Henry Ford Health System:
A 100 Year Legacy

Ready for Sea: The History
of the U.S. Navy Supply Corps

Dreamers & Builders:
The History of Zachry Corporation

Zachry Holdings, Inc.:
The First Ninety Years

Publisher's Cataloging-In-Publication Data
(Prepared by The Donohue Group, Inc.)

Names: Rodengen, Jeffrey L. | Campbell, Kim, 1964- editor. | Thompson, Darcey McNiff, designer.

Title: Nestlé in the United States : a celebration of good food, good life / Jeffrey L. Rodengen ; edited by Kim Campbell ; design and layout by Darcey McNiff Thompson.

Other Titles: Celebration of good food, good life

Description: Fort Lauderdale, FL : Write Stuff Enterprises, LLC, [2016] | Includes bibliographical references and index.

Identifiers: LCCN 2016936805 | ISBN 978-1-932022-66-7

Subjects: LCSH: Nestlé—History. | Food industry and trade— United States—History.

Classification: LCC HD9009.N47 R64 2016 | DDC 338.4/766400973—dc23

Please visit WriteStuff.com for a complete listing

Write Stuff Enterprises, LLC
1001 South Andrews Avenue
Fort Lauderdale, FL 33316
1-800-900-Book (1-800-900-2665)
(954) 462-6657
www.writestuffbooks.com
Since 1986

Completely produced in the United States of America

10 9 8 7 6 5 4 3 2 1

TABLE *of* CONTENTS

INTRODUCTION

Introduction by
PAUL GRIMWOOD
Chairman and CEO
Nestlé USA

As Nestlé®, SA, headquartered in Vevey, Switzerland, celebrates its worldwide 150th anniversary in 2016, I'm proud to share with you the amazing history of Nestlé right here in the United States. As market head of *Nestlé* in the US, I have the pleasure of representing eight *Nestlé* operating companies in America. Each has its own special history, and has made its own unique contribution to American society.

Taken together, the companies and products presented in this book represent more than 51,000 employees working in 179 locations in 47 states with nine research and development centers, making products at 87 factories that are dispersed throughout the country from five main distribution centers.

Nestlé brands and products have had a profound influence in America and are in an astonishing 97 percent of American homes. Many readers will learn for the first time how diversified the categories of *Nestlé* brands are in the United States.

Imagine a company that is among the top two suppliers in the categories of Pet Care, Confections, Frozen Food, Waters, Ice Cream, Nutrition, Coffee & Creamers, Baking, Ready-to-Drink Milk, and Skin Care. These categories represent the most universally known and beloved brands throughout the country, such as Gerber®, Carnation®, Nesquik®, Purina®, Friskies®, BOOST®, Nescafé®, Toll House®, Buitoni®, Perrier®, Arrowhead®, DiGiorno®, Baby Ruth®, Nestlé Crunch®, Häagen-Dazs®, Stouffer's®, Libby's®, Chef-mate®, Dysport®, and Cetaphil®—to name a few of the leading brands you will meet in the following pages.

It will also interest you to learn that many of the best-known consumer brands of today had their start in America long before they joined the *Nestlé* family.

Since the beginning of our collective global journey 150 years ago, we believe that to create value for our shareholders, we must create value for society. We embed that philosophy in everything we do. *Nestlé* is the largest purchaser of dairy ingredients in the US—buying $1 billion annually. We purchase more than 660 million pounds of fruit and vegetables each year.

As you read about the deep roots that many *Nestlé* brands have in American history, you will also learn that *Nestlé* takes a long-term view when it comes to setting our strategy. Across all the operating companies in the United States, *Nestlé* is investing heavily in research and technology because innovation and improvement are embedded in our DNA.

As the world's largest food and beverage company, *Nestlé* is committed to being a trusted leader in nutrition, health, and wellness. We are proud of our initiatives over the last 10 years to improve the quality of our products. Our efforts to reduce sugar, sodium, saturated fat, trans fats, artificial flavors, and Federal Drug Administration-certified colors from our products have positively affected millions of consumers. Our operating companies in the United States have made significant commitments to dramatically reduce carbon emissions by using sustainably managed renewable energy sources, using water-saving technology, and managing our distribution networks. We seek to bring about the change needed for the health of our planet and its inhabitants, both human and our pets.

So, on behalf of *Nestlé* employees across the United States, we thank you for your passionate support of *Nestlé* and hope that you and your family continue to enjoy our products.

ACKNOWLEDGMENTS

MANY DEDICATED INDIVIDUALS ASSISTED IN THE RESEARCH, preparation, and publication of this story of *Nestlé in the United States: A Celebration of Good Food, Good Life.*

Write Stuff is deeply grateful for the contributions and vision of Nestlé USA Chairman and CEO Paul Grimwood, who worked closely with the author to bring the rich and storied history of Nestlé in the United States to this book.

Research Assistants Torrey Kim and Sandy Smith conducted the principal archival research for the book, while Managing Editor Kim Campbell directed the editorial content. Graphic Designer Darcey McNiff Thompson brought the story to life.

Several key individuals with Nestlé provided their assistance in development of the book from its outline to its finished product, especially Molly Dell'Omo, who provided insight and guidance with grace and good humor at all hours.

Write Stuff would like to give special recognition to Nestlé employees Alexis Bergen, Nestlé USA; Sue Csuhran, Nestlé R&D Center Solon; and Marlin Ezell and Peter Gent, Nestlé USA.

Write Stuff is grateful to the assistance of Josh Lehman and Lily Stern, Galderma Laboratories, LP; Doreen Berlinghof and Mary Wade, Nestlé Health Science; Monique Britton and Allison Moore, Nespresso; Clare Argetsinger, Mariana Canale, Cathy Dunn, Shawn Gibbs, Ellen Keating, Maria Pontone, Jacqueline Stelling, and Bernadette Tortorella, Nestlé Nutrition; Laura Hardin, Nestlé Professional North America; Mark Pierce and Stacy Breihan, Nestlé Purina

PetCare Company; Angie Yoshimura and Hillary Fox, Nestlé USA; and Laura McCafferty and John Halloran, Nestlé Waters North America. In addition, Nicole Jordan and the staff at HeritageWerks, particularly Geoff Hetherington and Luis Rospigliosi, provided key research material from the Nestlé USA archives.

All of the individuals interviewed—Nestlé employees, retirees, and friends—were generous with their time and insights. Those who shared their memories and thoughts include Bill Biggar, Jim Biggar, Tim Brown, John Carmichael, Judy Cascapera, Rob Case, Louise DeFalco, Susanna Forteleoni, Jeff Hamilton, Laura Hardin, Kim Jeffery, Katerina Kakanas, Robert Kilmer, Bob Kosters, Nina Leigh Krueger, Jane Lazgin, Barbara McCartney, Pat McGinnis, Perry Miele, Anna Mohl, Maureen Monahan, Andrew Muniak, Virginie Naigeon, Dr. Juan Ochoa, Roz O'Hearn, Bill Partyka, James Pergola, Hyder Raheem, Keith Schopp, Carol Siegel, Joe Sivewright, Tom Smith, Eric Somnolet, Cam Starrett, Aileen Stocks, Carol Stropki, Patrick Todd, Carlos Velasco, John Vella, and Joe Weller.

Finally, special thanks are extended to the staff at Write Stuff Enterprises, LLC: Christian Ramirez and Larry Schwingel, senior editors; Sandy Cruz, senior vice president/creative services manager; Cristofer Valle, senior graphic designer and studio administrator; Sarah Alender, Eric Brown, Linda Dougherty, Connie Greenawald, Rick Hazeltine, Sannie Kirschner, Randy Laumann, Lisa McCoy, Christine McIntire, Nicole Sirdoreus, proofreaders; Patricia Dolbow and Barbara Martin, transcriptionists; Lisa Ryan, indexer; Amy Major, executive assistant to Jeffrey L. Rodengen; Marianne Roberts, president, publisher, and chief financial officer; and Norma Wolpin, marketing manager.

Nestlé

1866

Nestlé competitor the Anglo-Swiss Condensed Milk Company is founded by Americans Charles Page and his brothers after they purchase an evaporated milk factory in Cham, Switzerland.

1900

In Fulton, New York Nestlé opens its first factory in the United States. The milk plant later produces chocolate, and by 1951 becomes the largest of Nestlé's 17 worldwide chocolate factories.

1973

Nestlé acquires Stouffer's and with it, a reputation for made-from-scratch foods. The next year, Nestlé adds frozen French bread pizza to the product line.

1985

Nestlé acquires Carnation for $3 billion. The news makes headlines, as at the time it is the largest non-oil acquisition in history.

GOOD FOOD, GOOD LIFE

1992

Nestlé acquires Source Perrier, based in Paris, parent company of The Perrier Group of America. Years later, Nestlé rechristens the newly purchased group Nestlé Waters.

2001

Nestlé acquires Ralston Purina and moves its own pet care unit to St. Louis to be part of the newly created Nestlé Purina PetCare Company.

2007

Gerber joins Nestlé Nutrition as a global force to inspire parents everywhere to feed their children the healthiest foods possible.

2009

Nestlé holds its first annual Creating Shared Value Forum in New York, bringing together leading experts on nutrition, water, and rural development to discuss global challenges.

This page: Fresh milk arrives at The Anglo-Swiss Condensed Milk Company factory in Cham, Switzerland, in 1899. Nestlé and its Anglo-Swiss rivals would eventually merge in 1905.

Opposite: Henri Nestlé started his company in 1866 in Vevey, Switzerland, with his revolutionary infant formula.

NESTLÉ—A GLOBAL OVERVIEW

NESTLÉ IS A GLOBAL BRAND, AND much of its inspiration comes from iconic local brands: Perrier® from France, for instance, or the United Kingdom's Kit Kat® bar, or Swiss-made Cailler chocolate. But American brands and American inventors and innovators have long shaped Nestlé's global influences.

While the company bears the name of Henri Nestlé, it was a young American who laid the first stone in the company's foundation.

Charles Page became obsessed with the idea of canned milk while covering the Civil War for *The New York Times*. When he was sent to the US consul in Switzerland, he asked his brothers to join him; they did and purchased an evaporated milk factory.

The Anglo-Swiss Condensed Milk Company, founded in Cham in 1866, became one of Nestlé's greatest competitors before the two firms merged in 1905. But it also indirectly created one stateside competitor and directly influenced a future partner.

> *"The Nestlé story is amazing. What started in 1866 with Henri Nestlé has grown into the the world's largest food and beverage company."*
>
> **—PAUL GRIMWOOD**
> Chairman and CEO, Nestlé USA, Inc.

**Elbridge A. Stuart (inset),
who managed a grocery
store in El Paso, Texas (above),
purchased 100 cases
of Helvetia Milk Condensing
Company's canned milk for
his store. That fateful decision
would lead to Stuart forming
his own canned milk
company—Carnation.**

John Baptist Meyenberg, an Anglo-Swiss employee, suggested better canning methods. The Page brothers saw no need to change what was successful. Meyenberg emigrated to the United States and pursued his idea, eventually forming Helvetia Milk Condensing Company in 1890. It later became Pet Milk— both a competitor of and World War II-era partner to Carnation.

Helvetia also influenced Carnation founder Elbridge A. Stuart, who started the Pacific Coast Condensed Milk Company in 1899. He created condensed cream—later called condensed milk—that had a multitude of uses, from a simple beverage to baking and cooking.

After decades of competition, Nestlé and Anglo-Swiss merged in 1905. They were poised to seize upon opportunity when World War I began in Europe, which created shortages of raw materials but brought with it wartime contracts. Nestlé opened new factories and purchased several existing factories in the United States, its first presence in America. By the end of the war in 1918, there were 40 Nestlé factories worldwide.

Chocolate also traveled the US-Swiss connection. Peter's Chocolate— created by Daniel Peter—had a Nestlé influence as well. Peter had attempted to create a milk chocolate confection, something that his friend and neighbor Henri Nestlé was able to assist with. In 1908, Peter's opened its first US manufacturing plant in Fulton, NY. Lamont, Corliss & Company—a US sales representative for the company—purchased Peter's and in 1951 rebranded it Nestlé Chocolate Company.

The War Years: Stateside

Nestlé grew in the United States throughout the Great Depression, though it was difficult. The company added chocolate and beverages to its product lines. As the world again moved to war, the United States would once more play a critical role in the company's history. To make sure operations continued while the war devastated Europe, Nestlé moved its board of directors and general management team to the United States.

World War II influenced the Buitoni® brand, with prominent family members riding out the conflict in the United States. To survive, they introduced both *Buitoni* pasta and Perugina® chocolates to Americans. Nestlé acquired the companies in 1988.

The Second World War also served to introduce the Nescafé® brand to the United States. Servicemen had discovered the instant coffee brand while in Europe, and it soon became a popular way to drink coffee.

In the immediate aftermath of the war, the world economy boomed and Nestlé grew strategically by creating new products and purchasing others. Maggi® brand was a key acquisition in Switzerland in 1947. Nesquik®—originally called Quik—was developed in the United States in 1948.

Above: Henri Nestlé adapted his family coat of arms to create the company's original logo.

Left: Nescafé changed the way Americans drink coffee. Having good instant coffee encouraged the office coffee break and other social events with the product.

Below: Farfel the spokesdog's popularity with kids rivaled that of the drink itself.

Establishing New Market Opportunities: The 1950s and 1960s

In July 1950, Nestlé began construction on an 80,000-square-foot addition to its Fulton chocolate plant in New York, which would become the largest of Nestlé's 17 chocolate factories around the world.

As the new medium of television captured the imaginations of American consumer households in the 1950s, Nestlé embraced both print and television advertising to promote its growing portfolio of brands. In 1956, Nestlé introduced Farfel as the playful "spokesdog" for Quik chocolate milk mix. Farfel became among the most familiar brand spokesmen on both television and radio. Nestlé co-sponsored *The Lone Ranger*, then television's most popular half-hour daytime program for children. Farfel would remain Nestlé's iconic representative until his retirement in 1966.

Above: Nestlé Toll House Cookie Mix featured Nestlé Semi-Sweet Chocolate Morsels and was carefully kitchen-tested to help bakers make America's favorite cookies the quick and easy way.

Above: After Nestlé purchased Stouffer's in 1973, two iconic frozen food lines were developed: French bread pizza (1974) and Lean Cuisine (1981).

During the second half of the decade of the 1950s, Nestlé promotional campaigns focused on *Nescafé*, Nestea®, and Toll House® chocolate morsels. An indication of the continuing growth of the company, The Nestlé Company, which included Nestlé's Chocolate Company, built new corporate offices in White Plains, NY, which functioned as the company's American headquarters.

As the American space age took off in the 1960s, Nestlé collaborated with NASA to create special "space candy" for the long duration of the Gemini spaceflight, which provided both nutrition and great taste for astronauts. Nestlé also sponsored the traditional Thanksgiving Day parades on television, showcasing Farfel among the main attractions. By 1966, Nestlé had built the "world's largest instant tea plant" in Granite City, IL, along with "the world's most modern and best-automated chocolate plant" in Burlington, WI. During the decade, Nestlé slowly increased its percentage of ownership in canned food company Libby, McNeill & Libby until by 1970 it owned the majority of Libby's shares, and would own it outright by 1975.

The 1970s and 1980s: Significant Growth

By the 1970s, the world was changing. Women were in the workforce in larger numbers and family meals were different. Stouffer's—which joined Nestlé in 1973—capitalized on the trend. Stouffer's launched two iconic lines: Stouffer's® French bread pizza, created in 1974, and Lean Cuisine®, which joined the frozen food lineup in 1981.

Nestlé made its mark outside of food as well. In 1974, the company made its first non-food investment, purchasing a portion of cosmetic company L'Oréal. In 1976, it purchased Alcon Laboratories, the US maker of pharmaceuticals and ophthalmic products.

The company's acquisition of Carnation in 1985 completed the massive growth phase. That set in motion an exciting—and very successful—time for Nestlé. "It was a beautiful match for both," said Joe Weller, former CEO of Nestlé USA, Inc. "The business exploded after that. We had 10 years of unbelievable growth, and it was a great time for Nestlé in the USA."

Nestlé's growth was not limited to the United States, though. Italian firm Buitoni joined Nestlé in 1986 while Nespresso®—an exclusively European product at the time—launched in 1984. Both brands eventually joined the Nestlé US portfolio.

After the company had an opportunity to catch its breath from the growth, it opted to shift the US companies into one unit: Nestlé USA, Inc. was created in 1990, combining most of its food and beverage operations at the time under one umbrella.

In 1992, Nestlé purchased Source Perrier, based in Paris, parent company of The Perrier Group of America. Eventually, Nestlé renamed the newly purchased group Nestlé Waters.

Nestlé's acquisition of Carnation in 1985 led to explosive growth for the brand. Shown here, 1980s-era packaging for sweetened condensed milk.

All in the Family: The 1990s

In 1990 Nestlé named Timm Crull, who was then president of Carnation, CEO of Nestlé USA, Inc.. New leadership marked an opportunity for Nestlé to improve operations and to gain market share. At the time, the company's US operations generated $6 billion in sales, landing it in third place behind ConAgra and Kraft.

After the various organizations merged into one entity, all the businesses were brought under the Nestlé USA, Inc. umbrella. Those not directly food- or beverage-related—like the eye-care company Alcon and Perrier of America (soon renamed Nestlé Waters)—continued to operate as independent business units reporting to Switzerland.

Prior to the consolidation, "each of the businesses Nestlé acquired retained their management team, retained every aspect of how they managed their business, and retained most of the decision-making about their business," said Cam Starrett, head of human resources at Nestlé USA, Inc. during its formative years. "Once under the Nestlé USA, Inc. umbrella, the businesses worked together to become more efficient and share best practices and consumer insights."

"One of the cultural characteristics of Nestlé is this uniform agreement about quality and efficiency. Maybe those originally were Swiss strengths, but Nestlé in the United States has taken it to a whole new level," said Roz O'Hearn, director of communications and brand affairs for Nestlé USA, Inc.

The consolidation marked Nestlé's third business model change in 100 years of US operations. As it continued into the 1990s, the company purchased a number of new products and divested others.

Nestlé has installed solar power collection panels at many of its facilities worldwide. At its Purina facility in Flagstaff, Arizona, almost 2,000 panels collect solar energy for use at the plant.

"There is such a strong culture at Nestlé and that's reflected in the people we hire. Our employees are a huge competitive advantage."

—JUDY CASCAPERA
Chief People Officer (CPO)
Nestlé USA, Inc.

The Growth Continues: 2000 and Beyond

The dawn of the new century brought more growth for Nestlé. A number of ice cream brands, including Dreyer's® and Drumstick®, joined over the years. A merger with Ralston Purina aligned the US pet food maker with Carnation's Friskies® line. The companies fit well together, as their cultures shared many of the same values. Keith Schopp, vice president of corporate public relations, Nestlé Purina PetCare Company, North America, said, "Generally this is a company where people spend an entire career. It's not unusual to see people with more than 25 years of service. I think that really speaks to the culture and the kind of place this is."

Nestlé intensified its efforts in health and wellness with the acquisition of Wyeth Nutrition and the formation of Nestlé Health Science and the Nestlé Institute of Health Sciences. Nestlé Health Science then acquired Prometheus Laboratories and Pamlab. Gerber®, a baby food product with a long legacy, built on Nestlé's roots of creating products for infants. Nestlé Skin Health was created to focus on the rapidly growing skin health sector.

As the company grew, Nestlé kept its focus on the consumer. "Nestlé has an extensive research network, which allows us to gather and analyze consumer trends and insights," Laura Hardin, corporate communications manager for Nestlé Professional, said. "We're interested in what consumers are seeing, what they're buying, and what they are eating at home and at restaurants. At Nestlé Professional, we work with operators to deliver the flavor and quality consumers want."

But in its legacy brands, consumers' tastes changed. Water—driven significantly by Nestlé Waters' lineup—was poised to overtake soft drinks as the leading national beverage. Nestlé removed artificial flavors from its frozen lines and added more nutritious vegetables. Nestlé focused on protecting resources and improving the quality of life in the communities in which it operates.

Nestlé Growth In the USA

Nestlé grew steadily from its formative years. Today, the United States is Nestlé's largest market in the world. In 2015, Nestlé product sales totaled $26 billion, and 97 percent of US households purchased Nestlé products. Nestlé in the US consists of eight separate businesses: Nestlé USA, Inc., Nestlé Waters North America, Nestlé Purina PetCare, Nestlé Nutrition, Nestlé Health Science, Nestlé Professional, Nestlé Skin Health, and Nespresso. These organizations operate 87 factories in 47 states and represent more than 51,000 employees.

"At Nestlé, we know that as the world's largest food and beverage company, we have an opportunity to create immense positive impact," Paul Grimwood, chairman and CEO of Nestlé USA, Inc., explained. "For the past 10 years we have worked to reduce sugar, sodium, and saturated fat and remove trans fat from our products, without sacrificing taste, positively impacting millions of consumers striving for better health and balanced diets."

Celebrating Nestlé's acquisition of Purina in 2001 are (left to right): John Harris, former president of Friskies PetCare, Joe Weller, former chairman and CEO of Nestlé USA, Inc., and Pat McGinnis, former CEO of Purina.

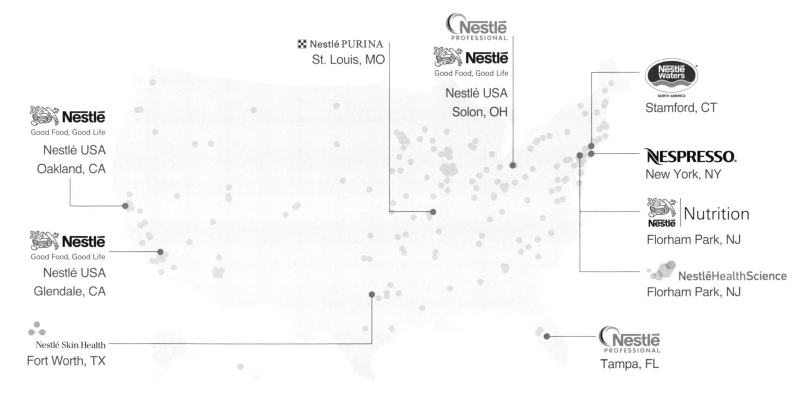

The Nestlé factory in Modesto, California, produces products for both the United States and Puerto Rico. In 2015, Nestlé transformed the factory into a "zero water" plant to reduce the amount of water it uses in California.

Creating Shared Value

Nestlé's 150th anniversary represents a significant milestone in many dimensions. Nestlé understands that to prosper it must take a long-term view, framed in a robust set of principles and values developed over the last 150 years. "Our commitments are based on values that form the foundation upon which we build our actions in Creating Shared Value," Grimwood said. This key Nestlé conviction extends to shareholders, consumers, employees, suppliers, and to the broader communities where Nestlé has a significant presence.

Among the important categories directly affected by the philosophy are environmental sustainability, such as ongoing efforts to conserve water across all Nestlé business units through advanced technologies and water stewardship. Water is vital to Nestlé operations, used for washing and processing raw materials, cooling and cleaning equipment, hygiene, and the company's bottled water business. Nestlé also supports a goal of zero waste to landfills at its factories. Nestlé has adopted new and more efficient technologies and processes and by the end of 2015, 35 of its factories in the United States achieved landfill-free status.

Nestlé in the US is committed to being a trusted leader in Nutrition, Health & Wellness. Nestlé's diverse portfolio of products provides nutritious options and healthy choices for every member of the family at every stage of life. More and more, consumers' tastes and preferences are changing, along with what they define as relevant. Nestlé continues to develop new recipes and update existing ones across its entire portfolio to simplify ingredient lists while maintaining the same great tastes consumers have grown to love. Recent innovations include gluten-free products, those made with organic ingredients, and the removal of artificial flavors. Nestlé also removed artificial colors, adding colors from natural sources when needed.

The lives of our pets are also very important. Nestlé Purina is dedicated to improving the lives of pets by providing healthy, 100% complete and balanced pet foods backed by exceptional science and nutritional expertise. More than 500 Nestlé Purina nutritionists, behaviorists, veterinarians, immunologists, and other pet experts use their expertise daily to enrich our knowledge of pet nutrition and care. Nestlé works hard to help pets live longer, healthier lives by moving nutrition forward in the areas of healthy aging, healthy metabolism, oral health, microbiome digestive health, healthy early development, and well-being.

Each of the eight Nestlé operating companies receives its own spotlight in the chapters to follow. But Creating Shared Value has a special meaning for Nestlé's relationship with the entire Nestlé family of employees. Nestlé has long recognized that employees are a key source of its competitive advantage, and their efforts elevate Nestlé as the premier choice for top diverse talent in the United States. As Nestlé grows and adapts, the company also works hard to foster a culture of wellness among employees. Nestlé offers employees best-in-class health plans with additional benefits, a Health Savings Plan, and a tobacco cessation program. Nestlé recognizes that safety and health are important for everyone at Nestlé, regardless of what they do or where they work. "Nestlé's most important assets are our people," Paul Grimwood shared, "which is why the safety and health of our employees are our top priorities."

As Nestlé celebrates its 150th anniversary, it does so as a global leader in food and beverages and a leader on issues of sustainability and the environment.

Said Grimwood: "Our Creating Shared Value efforts focus on Nutrition, Health & Wellness, environmental impact, and social impact."

It is Nestlé's focus on consumers—and their well-being—that continues to drive Nestlé today.

Above: Nestlé's focus on Nutrition, Health and Wellness benefits every member of the family.

Below: In July 2015, Nestlé partnered with Boys & Girls Clubs of America to launch the National Fitness Competition in Cleveland, Ohio.

Nestlé

1867

Swiss pharmacist Henri Nestlé creates his "Farine Lactée" product, which combines cow's milk, wheat flour, and sugar as a nutritional source for infants.

1927

Young mother Dorothy Gerber stands in her Fremont, Michigan kitchen struggling to strain solid foods to feed her daughter. Her husband Dan suggests he can strain fruits and vegetables at his canning business, Fremont Canning Company, sparking the beginning of Gerber Baby Foods.

1939

Gerber introduces its first baby cereal.

1988

Nestlé launches its formula line in the United States under the name Carnation Good Start.

2001

Gerber launches its aseptic journey with the introduction of 15 2nd Foods fruits in the Fremont, Michigan facility. Over the next year, Gerber introduces 10 1st Foods fruit and vegetable items, making it the first company in the United States to produce and market aseptic low-acid foods (vegetables) for infants.

2002

Gerber conducts the United States' first Feeding Infants and Toddlers Study (FITS) to evaluate the eating patterns and nutrient intake of more than 3,200 infants and toddlers.

2007

Gerber joins Nestlé Nutrition as a global force to inspire parents everywhere to feed their children the healthiest foods possible.

2011

Gerber successfully petitions the US Food and Drug Administration to accept the first qualified health claim for infant formula.

THE FORMULA FOR A GREAT START TO LIFE

ALTHOUGH HENRI NESTLÉ MAY HAVE BEEN TOO HUMBLE TO HAVE trumpeted his accomplishments, the reality is that he was one of the pioneers who helped reduce the infant mortality rate in 19th-century Europe. Nestlé's research on how to best nourish babies led to innovations that were major milestones in the baby formula, cereal, and food category. The company continues to build on that foundation today through its Gerber® Good Start® and *Gerber Baby Food* product lines, which allow children to thrive by helping them meet their nutritional needs.

Opposite: Gerber offers many products that provide proper nutrition for infants.

Right: In 1867, pharmacist Henri Nestlé created his "Farine Lactée," which was the beginning of the Nestlé company.

Humble Beginnings

Henri Nestlé was a pharmacist in Vevey, Switzerland, by trade, a job that gave him a firsthand view of exactly which products needed innovation to help save lives. By the late 1860s, Nestlé knew that the issue of child nutrition was crucial—at that time, one in every five European children did not live to his or her first birthday.

One of the biggest impediments to infant survival was a lack of alternative feeding methods when children couldn't breastfeed. Although porridge was an option at the time, it wasn't formulated for infants' sensitive digestive tracts and often led to intestinal disorders that could be fatal in babies. This led Nestlé to create his "Farine Lactée" product, which combined cow's milk, wheat flour, and sugar as a nutritional source for infants. While Nestlé was still testing the product, a colleague told him about a premature baby who had been vomiting for two weeks, unable to digest mother's milk or any alternatives. Nestlé put a diluted version of his infant "soup" into a bottle and fed it to the baby. The child recovered within a few days.

Word quickly spread about the child's amazing recovery thanks to Nestlé's cereal, and doctors began recommending it. Just four years after feeding it to that sick infant, Nestlé's baby formula won the first gold medal at the 1871 World Exhibition for its role in reducing the infant mortality rate. Yet Nestlé remained humble about his innovation, saying, "My invention is not a new discovery but a correct and rational application of substances long known to be the best for the feeding of children. The chief ingredients are quality milk, bread, and sugar."

Above: The Pharmacie Centrale in Vevey, Switzerland, seen here in 1900, where Henri Nestlé (inset) worked from 1839–1843.

Below right: Henri Nestlé's infant formula advertised in German.

Below: An early container of Henri Nestlé's "Farine Lactée."

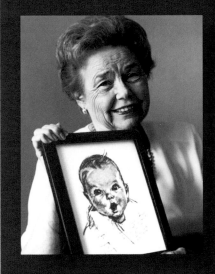

Dorothy Gerber Takes the Next Step

About a half-century after Nestlé's groundbreaking discovery, a young mother named Dorothy Gerber stood in her Fremont, Michigan kitchen straining solid foods to feed her daughter, which proved to be a frustrating process. Her husband Dan suggested that he could more easily strain fruits and vegetables at his canning business, and after he was able to create baby food at work, several employees started asking him to do the same for their children—sparking the beginning of *Gerber* Baby Foods.

Gerber's business took off, but no matter how big the company grew, Dan Gerber always felt a strong responsibility and commitment to his youngest customers. A picture of Dan Gerber shows how connected he was with the consumer. He is turning the soil of a new manufacturing site surrounded by—not the mayor and a marching band—but little kids who came out with their trowels, and they were turning the soil with him.

Because both Nestlé and Gerber had such rich histories feeding children, it seemed like a natural marriage to join the two businesses. In 2007, Gerber joined Nestlé Nutrition as a global force that would inspire parents everywhere to feed their children the healthiest foods possible.

Above: Gerber launched a competition in 1928 in search of a baby whose face would represent the company in advertisements and on the jars of baby food. The winning drawing of Ann Turner Cook has appeared on all of Gerber's packaging and ads since 1931.

Left: Pictured is the original factory building in Fremont, Michigan, as it was in 1928. This is the site of the current factory.

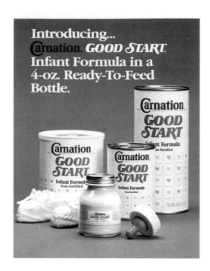

Above: Nestlé first launched infant formulas in the United States in 1988 under the Carnation Good Start brand. Now called Gerber Good Start (right), these formulas continue to build on the heritage of providing appropriate nutrition for infant growth and development.

Below right: Gerber's Good Start milk-based infant formula continues to contain a 100 percent partially hydrolyzed whey protein that supports easy digestion. Nestlé continues to provide babies "a nutritious alternative to breast milk," said Robyn Wimberly, manager for medical marketing.

A Strong Formula

Although Nestlé has offerings to help children thrive at any age, the first product that most babies encounter is the company's infant formula, *Gerber Good Start*.

"If moms only knew what we know about our formula, they would see that we believe we have the best formula out there," said Aileen Stocks, chief marketing officer for Infant Nutrition North America. "Our infant formulas are backed by decades of scientific research and clinical trials in collaboration with leading experts in the field of infant nutrition. If mom cannot or chooses not to breastfeed, we want to make sure that we give her an offer that's modeled after breast milk, and we believe that *Good Start* has that."

The cutting-edge technology behind Carnation® *Good Start* was extraordinary. The formula was made with 100 percent whey protein, partially hydrolyzed, or broken down, into smaller pieces to be well tolerated and easy to digest. These proteins were later called Comfort Proteins® and were at the heart of what made this new formula truly different in the marketplace. Over the years, clinical studies have demonstrated that formulas made from 100 percent whey protein, partially hydrolyzed, may help reduce the risk of infants developing atopic dermatitis, the most common allergy of infancy. "The Food and Drug Administration authorized a qualified health claim for the relationship between Nestlé's partially hydrolyzed 100 percent whey protein and the risk reduction of

atopic dermatitis in infants with a family history of allergy when fed for the first four months of life, as compared to intact cows milk protein,"* said Eric Somnolet, vice president, infant formula, for North America. "The *Gerber* brand brings us immediate, broad awareness as an infant nutrition expert."

A second competitive advantage, Somnolet says, is the company's relationship with consumers: "Gerber has a capacity and understanding for speaking directly to moms." Another natural advantage that Gerber has in the formula category is that it focuses on quality at every level of the organization. "Quality isn't only in our factories," Somnolet said. "Quality is all along the supply chain, through product distribution to product consumption. It is extraordinary to see the lengths to which we go to ensure product quality. If anyone knows quality in infant formulas, it is Gerber."

*For healthy infants who are not exclusively breastfed and who have a family history of allergy, feeding a 100% whey protein partially hydrolyzed infant formula from birth up to 4 months of age instead of a formula containing intact cow's milk proteins may reduce the risk of developing atopic dermatitis throughout the first year of life. FDA has concluded that the relationship between 100% whey protein partially hydrolyzed infant formulas and the reduced risk of atopic dermatitis is uncertain, because there is little scientific evidence for the relationship.

Partially hydrolyzed formulas **should not be fed to infants who are allergic to milk or to infants with existing milk allergy symptoms.** If you suspect your baby is already allergic to milk, or if your baby is on a special formula for the treatment of allergy, your baby's care and feeding choices should be under a doctor's supervision.

Gerber Life Means Financial Protection

GERBER LIFE OFFERS insurance to families and businesses. "We're the number one juvenile life insurance company in the United States," explained Keith O'Reilly, president and CEO of Gerber Life Insurance Company. "Families trust the Gerber name."

The company's suite of products includes the Grow Up® Plan, *Gerber* Life College Plan, Term Life plan, Whole Life, Guaranteed Life insurance plan, and Accident Protection plan. *Gerber* Life Insurance has been in business for almost 50 years and has three and a half million policyholders.

Above: In 2015, Gerber debuted its Lil' Bits recipes, which includes soft, bite-sized foods so babies can learn how to chew their foods. The company invested more than $100 million in the technology required to create the products.

Above right: Nestlé is committed to quality in its fruit and vegetable products from their beginning. The company has partnered with some farms for four generations. Many farmers maintain separate vegetable fields for Gerber products because Gerber sets such high quality standards.

Providing Proper Nutrition at Every Stage

In 2002, Gerber conducted the United States' first Feeding Infants and Toddlers Study (FITS). The study examined the diet and lifestyle behaviors of young children compared to recommendations and to determine where there was room for improvement.

In 2008, Gerber expanded the next FITS to reexamine the diets of infants and toddlers, and evaluated the diets of preschoolers. The latest study (FITS 2016) will continue to build on this body of research.

Findings from the FITS are published in peer-reviewed scientific journals and shared with key nutrition authorities, such as the FDA, the US Department of Agriculture, and the American Academy of Pediatrics, who establish public policy and nutrition recommendations for children.

FITS has unveiled many shocking realities when it comes to young children's diets. Although the company knew there was likely room for improvement, it was surprising to learn facts such as roughly one-third of infants, toddlers, and preschoolers do not eat a distinct portion of vegetables in a given day, and many others still fall short of the goal amounts each day. Sadly, French fries are the most commonly consumed vegetable for toddlers.

"We've taken these alarming statistics to heart and have renovated our product offerings to help children get more high-quality vegetables, whether at a meal or with our on-the-go snack options," said Bill Partyka, Regional Business Head, Nestlé Nutrition, NA. "That also influenced a lot of our product offerings," he added. "Gerber found strategic ways to unobtrusively tuck away vegetables in some of its snacks, and helps introduce more vegetables into babies' diets."

Gerber focused on the importance of the first 1,000 days with its Start Healthy, Stay Healthy™ initiative and the importance of establishing healthy eating habits from the start. FITS indicated that eating patterns

Key insights from FITS helped inform *Gerber*'s *Start Healthy, Stay Healthy* initiative. Gerber was the first to transition from an age-based feeding approach to one that is centered on developmental milestones, recognizing that needs differ as children move from sitting to crawling to walking.

Gerber has worked to remove artificial colors, flavors, and sweeteners in its products, including snacks and foods made especially for children.

are established as early as 12 months and are fairly set by 24 months. "In other words, the types of foods children eat as they transition to table food mirror the unhealthy eating habits of older children and adults, such as lower fruits and vegetables and higher sweets and grains," said Stocks. "We've taken this to heart and renovated some of toddlers' favorite foods to help with these gaps. For instance, butternut squash is now blended into our Gerber Lil' Meals™ Mac & Cheese with Chicken & Vegetables to help deliver vegetables in a tasty and kid-friendly way."

Gerber offers its free MyGerber program to parents who want advice on the best menus for their kids, as well as a growth tracker and educational advice for parents.

Beyond Products

In addition to Gerber's famous line of formula and baby foods, the company offers services such as its Parent Resource Center, which employs about 60 people who help ease the minds of new parents. This includes a 24/7 parent hotline so parents can call and ask any questions they have. Gerber

Baby food donated by Gerber arrives in Haiti for people affected by the 2010 earthquake.

A Spirit of Giving

EVER SINCE DAN GERBER ESTABLISHED THE GERBER BABY FOODS FUND in 1952, Gerber has been a leader in supporting the success of children all over the world. Now known as The Gerber Foundation, the organization carries on Dan Gerber's initial goal of ensuring that the company gives back to the community. Responding to what children need after tragedies and emergencies is chief among Gerber's altruistic goals. "We provide relief for babies and children who are in need of humanitarian help," said Aileen Stocks, chief marketing officer for Infant Nutrition North America. The company has given grants, food, and other gifts in support of relief efforts worldwide.

Gerber maintains a partnership with Feeding America to show parents the best ways to ensure that their children receive optimal nutrition. "We're looking at some of these areas where the need is greatest, focusing on some urban areas and true food deserts, to teach mom how to provide the right nutrition for her children," Stocks said.

Embracing the Environment

FEEDING BABIES AND CHILDREN MAKES A VAST IMPACT ON PEOPLE ALL OVER the world, but Gerber also works hard to ensure that the company makes a positive environmental impact as well.

Making baby food uses a lot of water while growing the fruits and vegetables, then washing them after they're harvested, and finally for cooking them. But Nestlé has found ways to perform groundwater redistribution so the water is recycled at many of the farms where the food is grown. The company also seeks more sustainable packaging options for its products to reduce the impact on the environment.

Spray irrigates a growing crop of corn at Gerber's Fremont Factory Wastewater Management Facility, using treated and recycled wastewater from the baby food production factory.

has registered dietitians, lactation specialists, and even a sleep consultant on the line, so parents can receive expert answers at any hour of the day. To help make certain that kids are eating a balanced diet, the company created its MyGerber program, a guided nutrition program with education, services, and tools that grow with parents as their child grows.

Gerber also maintains a state-of-the-art Product Technology Center. This center is a global hub for technology support for baby food, providing technical assistance anywhere in the world as required for other factories. The US Gerber plants are known for their high-tech aseptic filling processes, which allow for the sterile and safe packaging of the company's products.

Gerber has forged a partnership with the American Academy of Pediatrics, and the two powerhouses work together on the Healthy Childhood Weight Initiative to improve health outcomes for children and reduce obesity rates, all of which can be affected by what a baby eats during his or her first 1,000 days of life. "It's an amazing place to work because the science continues to get more robust, and it tells us more and more: If you get the nutrition right in that early stage of life, you will reduce the risk of health issues later in life," Partyka said.

Isla, the winner of the 2015 Gerber Baby Photo search, continues a legacy started in 1928, when artist Dorothy Hope Smith submitted a sketch of Ann Turner Cook in a contest to be the face of the Gerber brand.

Looking Ahead

As Nestlé celebrates its 150th anniversary, Gerber has launched a completely renovated line of formula products, numbered with stages one through three, to mark the event. In addition, the Gerber food line continues to grow with the same quality ingredients and processes that Dan and Dorothy Gerber used to launch the company in 1927.

"Every year, moms exit the category, and a whole new crop of moms come in, and we're staying relevant with every generation," Stocks said.

1867

In Switzerland, Daniel Peter—working with his neighbor, Henri Nestlé—discovers a way to combine sweetened condensed milk with cocoa powder to create milk chocolate. Consumers worldwide immediately embrace the innovative confection.

1900

Nestlé opens its first factory in the United States in Fulton, New York, with an investment of $150,000. The plant produces baby food, condensed milk, and cheese until 1907, when it begins producing chocolate due to high consumer demand.

1938

The American love affair with chocolate deepens with the launch of Nestlé Crunch this year. The company's Fulton, New York plant churns out hundreds of thousands of bars of world-famous Nestlé Milk Chocolate and crisped rice.

1990

Nestlé buys Baby Ruth and Butterfinger from RJR Nabisco. Shortly after, Nestlé launches a Butterfinger ad featuring Bart Simpson giving the tagline: "Nobody better lay a finger on my Butterfinger."

2011

Skinny Cow brand snacks debuts, offering Dreamy Clusters and Heavenly Crisp bars for chocolate lovers who know looking good and staying healthy doesn't mean a life without indulgences.

2013

MAY
Nestlé announces its Cocoa Plan, which seeks to enable farmers to run profitable farms; improve social conditions; and source good quality, sustainable cocoa for Nestlé products.

2014

FEBRUARY 2
For the first time, Nestlé launches a new product during the Super Bowl. Butterfinger Peanut Butter Cups are introduced to the public during a 30-second TV commercial broadcast watched by an estimated 108 million people.

2015

FEBRUARY
Nestlé announces that it is removing all artificial colors and flavors from its chocolate products, making it the first major confections manufacturer to do so.

SATISFYINGLY SWEET

EVER SINCE HENRI NESTLÉ AND DANIEL PETER JOINED FORCES IN 1867 to create milk chocolate, the mere mention of the Nestlé name gets mouths watering. The company, long known for its chocolates, candies, snacks, and other treats, is a familiar name in the US confection category, all thanks to a strong commitment to quality ingredients and carefully selected acquisitions.

Nestlé's storied history in the chocolate industry started when Daniel Peter pondered how he could differentiate his chocolate brand from the competing brands throughout his native Switzerland. Working with his neighbor, Henri Nestlé, Peter discovered a way to combine sweetened condensed milk with cocoa powder to create milk chocolate, which consumers immediately embraced worldwide. Peter established a milk chocolate manufacturing facility in the United States in 1901, and by 1951, Peter's Chocolate was merged into Nestlé's Chocolate Company, bringing the company's history full circle.

Opposite: The first Nestlé factory in the United States, located in Fulton, New York, was known to many as The Chocolate Works. It opened in late 1900 with about 80 employees to produce baby food, condensed milk, and cheese. The factory first made chocolate in 1907, developing into a center of excellence for chocolate manufacturing until its doors closed in 2003.

Right: Nestlé store display, circa 1950s–1960s.

Top: This ad from 1939 declares the Nestlé Crunch bar a "Four Star Hit," an accurate description of the candy bar's popularity.

Above: Ventriloquist Jimmy Nelson along with (left to right) "Danny O'Day" and Farfel, the dog. Farfel helped sing the theme song for Nestlé chocolate.

Crossing the Atlantic

Although milk chocolate may have had European roots, chocolate and confections exploded across the United States in the early 1900s, and Nestlé's presence in the country would help the company become a mainstay in the category. By 1919, Nestlé was selling its Milk Chocolate® and Milk Chocolate with Almonds® bars in the United States amidst increasing demand for the creamy flavors. Nestlé followed the popularity of these confections with its Nestlé Crunch® bar in 1938, which featured crisped rice coated in smooth milk chocolate. Priced at just five cents, the *Crunch* bar became a favorite indulgence of Americans emerging from the depths of the Great Depression with new hopes for the future.

Unfortunately for those who wanted to get their hands on a Nestlé® chocolate bar, the development of transportation systems wasn't quite as swift as the evolution of chocolate products. Prior to World War I, Nestlé delivered its chocolates across the United States by railroad, followed by local deliveries using horse-drawn vans. "In New York, for example, teams of two and three of the heavy, powerful steeds pulled Nestlé wagons through the cobblestoned streets," the company later wrote.

Chocolate as a War Ration

DURING WORLD WAR II, NESTLÉ DEBUTED ITS "CHOCOLATE IS A Fighting Food!" campaign, delivering millions of chocolate bars to soldiers abroad as part of their rations. Nestlé's sales doubled between 1938 and 1945 thanks to the popularity of the company's chocolate bars during the war. By the end of World War II, chocolate and cocoa makers discovered that the world's cocoa supply was not able to keep up with the demand that had grown over the years, prompting Nestlé executives to conduct research and cross the globe in search of new cocoa sources. By 1955, Americans consumed approximately 30 percent of the world's cocoa but didn't produce any, so Nestlé's research in seeking cocoa sources was extremely valuable in maintaining production.

Nestlé included several of its products, including its iconic Crunch bar, in the US military's war rations during World War II.

Baby Ruth and Butterfinger packaging from the 1960s, when they were owned by the Curtiss Candy Company. The Oh Henry! packaging shown is from the 1970s.

Marketing Efforts Pay Off

While the company focused some of its efforts on production, it didn't ignore the power of marketing. Some seven years before the fictional Willy Wonka ran a contest to promote his candy company, Nestlé led the charge with an innovative contest. In 1957, *Nestlé* chocolate bars flew off the shelves thanks to the company's partnership with the Lone Ranger as part of its "Name the Pony" chocolate bar contest, with 15 Shetland ponies as the top prize. "The pony contest was so successful that it is now being repeated; pretty soon, there'll be another set of happy winners astride their golden-maned Shetland ponies—and lots more extra sales of chocolate bars for Nestlé," the company said. Nestlé launched its $100,000 Bar in 1966, featuring chocolate, caramel, and crispy rice separated into two small bars within one package. In 1984, the company changed the bar's name to the simpler 100 Grand®. That same year, Nestlé acquired Oh Henry!®, Sno-Caps®, Goobers®, Raisinets®, Bit-O-Honey, and Chunky® from Ward-Johnston. Just five years later, in 1989, Nestlé acquired the Baby Ruth® and Butterfinger® brands from RJR Nabisco, rounding out its already impressive collection of chocolate offerings.

Goobers (far left and top) were first introduced in 1929 by the Blumenthal Chocolate Company, which Nestlé acquired in 1984. The candy features peanuts dipped into milk chocolate and has been a popular movie theater snack since its debut.

Raisinets (near left and bottom) first hit the market in 1927, and consumers immediately took a liking to the milk chocolate-covered raisins, which had a delightful chewy texture.

CHUNKY'S BACK...WITH $4.00 OFF RED SOX TICKETS!
Up to $16 in Savings!

Just send 10 Chunky® wrappers and a ticket stub from any Boston Red Sox game for each rebate requested along with the completed certificate below. Chunky® will send you a $4 cash rebate for each request up to a total of $16!

SPECIAL EVENT! ■ Come join us for Chunky®/Red Sox Painters Hat Night on June 30th, when the Red Sox take on the Toronto Blue Jays at Fenway Park.

Chunky's partnership with Major League Baseball team the Boston Red Sox [above] allowed the company to create a following among sports fans. *Chunky* bars are thick but not long, so they are able to fit right into a consumer's palm, making them popular items nestled next to cash registers [above right] all over the country.

NESTLÉ's New $100,000 Bar

Tastes so good it's almost illegal

Chewy smooth caramel crisp
...covered with delicious Nestlé's chocolate

Right: Nestlé used an innovative technique to advertise the $100,000 bar when it debuted in 1966, with its tag line: "Tastes so good it's almost illegal."

Left: In 1984, Nestlé simplified the name of its iconic bar to "100 Grand."

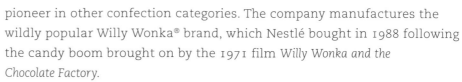

Beyond Chocolate

Although chocolate may make the world go around for many consumers, Nestlé is also a pioneer in other confection categories. The company manufactures the wildly popular Willy Wonka® brand, which Nestlé bought in 1988 following the candy boom brought on by the 1971 film *Willy Wonka and the Chocolate Factory*.

Wonka's most iconic brands include Laffy Taffy®, Spree®, SweeTARTS®, Nerds®, Wonka® Chocolate, Lik-M-Aid® Fun Dip, Pixy Stix®, Bottlecaps®, Kazoozles®, Runts®, and the infamous Everlasting Gobstopper®.

Pixy Stix (above) were originally conceived as a flavoring to mix into drinks, but kids liked the flavor so much that they started eating it straight from the straw. Wonka brand candies became immensely popular following the success of the 1971 film that profiled Charlie Bucket after he won an elusive "Golden Ticket" (above right). Nerds (near right) won the title of "Candy of the Year" in 1985, shortly after it debuted, and has been popular ever since. The Everlasting Gobstopper (far right) is another well-known brand in the Nestlé portfolio.

SweeTARTS (top left) were born in the 1960s using the same formula that Sunline, Inc. had created to make its Pixy Stix and Lik-M-Aid products. Sunline was later sold to Nestlé, and the company incorporated SweeTARTS into its Wonka line of products. Runts (top right) feature five different flavors in each box, including banana, orange, strawberry, green apple, and grape—but seasonal and special flavors often join the mix. Spree candies (middle left) have been on shelves since the 1960s, but when Nestlé acquired the brand, the company rolled them into its Wonka category. Lik-M-Aid (middle right) hit shelves in the 1940s and was later rebranded as Fun Dip. Laffy Taffy candies (left) feature flavored taffy confections accompanied by jokes that kids can read on the candy's wrapper.

It's Raining Chocolate

IT SOUNDS LIKE A CHOCOHOLIC'S FANTASY, BUT THERE REALLY WAS A TIME when chocolate fell from the sky.

In the early part of the 20th century, competition for candy bar sales was serious. Manufacturers wanted to make their products stand out, and they used marketing to do that.

Otto Schnering, the founder of the Curtiss Candy Company of Chicago, sold a chocolate bar with nuts called the Kandy Kake. Later he renamed it the Baby Ruth® after adding peanuts and nougat. Although some people maintain that Schnering named the candy bar after baseball great Babe Ruth, he swore in court that it was named after President Grover Cleveland's daughter Ruth. When Babe Ruth endorsed a competing candy bar, Curtiss Candy sued the company and won.

To get some attention for the new candy bar, Schnering chartered a plane and arranged for *Baby Ruth* bars to be tossed out of a plane over the city of Pittsburgh. The crowd below—especially the children—were delighted. The city of Pittsburgh was reportedly less enthused about a plane flying so low. Schnering arranged to duplicate the stunt in other cities nationwide, sending the bars down attached to tiny parachutes.

Above: Contrary to popular belief, Baby Ruth was not named after legendary baseball player Babe Ruth. Instead, the chocolate-covered peanut bar was named after President Grover Cleveland's daughter Ruth.

Below: The Baby Ruth candy bar came into existence in 1921, when it was manufactured and shipped out of this factory in Chicago.

Forging Ahead

With its roots deeply ingrained in American history, Nestlé is never content to simply rest on its stellar name—the company is always debuting new and innovative products that will continue to transform the confection industry. In September of 2015, Nestlé USA, Inc. entered the super-premium chocolate category by introducing 200-year-old Swiss chocolate brand Cailler into the US market.

The company also reinforced its standing as a steward of the community by being the first major confections manufacturer to announce the removal of all artificial flavors and FDA-certified colors from its chocolate candy products manufactured in the United States in 2015. For the first time in history, products like *Butterfinger*, *Crunch*, and *Baby Ruth* bars feature "No Artificial Flavors or Colors" notations on their packaging. "Our quality begins with the sourcing of all the raw materials," explained Louise DeFalco, former vice president of Technical and Production for Confections and Global Foods in Glendale, California. "Whether it's sugar or cocoa, we make sure that the product has no residual heavy metals, pesticides, etc. When it comes into our factories, it's then retested."

Nestlé is committed even further. The company's three-pillar Cocoa Plan™ includes support for all elements that bring the cocoa to Nestlé facilities: better farming, better cocoa, and better lives. Nestlé is committed to increasing its already existing portfolio of cocoa products that are "UTZ Certified," meaning Nestlé cocoa products will be more and more made with cocoa that is certified by an independent international non-profit to be responsibly sourced. Nestlé also helped found the World Cocoa Foundation, which provides, among its other programs, schools and teachers in cocoa-producing communities.

It's all part of Nestlé USA, Inc.'s commitment to "Good Food, Good Life" within its confections category.

> *"When you make a commitment, you have to readjust your recipes very carefully so that they match consumers' expectations."*
>
> **—CARLOS VELASCO**
> **President of the Confections & Global Foods Division of Nestlé USA, Inc.**

Above: In 2015, Nestlé brought Cailler super-premium chocolate products to the United States from Switzerland.

Left: Nestlé reinforced its standing as a steward of the community by being the first major confections manufacturer to remove all artificial flavors and FDA-certified colors from its chocolate candy products.

✓ **No Artificial** Flavors or Colors

Good results e

Carnati

'From Cor

Just Pure Milk
~evaporated to
double richness

1868

With $3,000 and a vision, Libby, McNeill & Libby is founded in Chicago, Illinois. Its first product is beef in brine, also known as corned beef.

1899

Elbridge A. Stuart founds Pacific Coast Condensed Milk Company with partner Tom Yerxa.

1902

E. A. Stuart automates his canning process. A century later, modern machinery continues to pack his evaporated milk product.

1929

Libby's purchases Dickinson & Company, acquiring its pumpkin-packing plant in Morton, Illinois. Today, the plant grows and processes 85 percent of the world's canned pumpkins.

1938

The Toll House Chocolate Crunch Cookie makes its first appearance in print in the 1938 edition of *Ruth Wakefield's Toll House Tried and True Recipes*. On March 20, 1939, Wakefield sells Nestlé the right to use her cookie recipe and the Toll House name … for $1.

1976

Nestlé purchases Libby's, the world's premier canned pumpkin producer. Less than a decade later, the purchase of Carnation by Nestlé and its Evaporated Milk product will bring two key pumpkin pie ingredients under one roof.

1985

The acquisition of Carnation by Nestlé makes headlines. At the time, the $3 billion deal is the largest non-oil acquisition in history.

1993

Nestlé makes having hot, delicious Toll House cookies even easier with the launch of refrigerated cookie dough.

IN THE PANTRY
AND IN THE OVEN

Nestlé products have become deeply ingrained in American daily life and special occasions. What would Thanksgiving be without a pumpkin pie made with Libby's® canned pumpkin and Carnation® Evaporated Milk? What would childhood be without sweet memories of baking Nestlé® Toll House® cookies with your family? Each of these iconic brands may have a familiar place on the family table, but the process of combining them into the Nestlé family has taken decades. Nestlé and Carnation, in particular, had grown alongside each other for many years, following similar business strategies and acquisitions. It wasn't until 1985 that the two aligned, creating a powerhouse brand.

Opposite: Carnation, along with other manufacturers, sponsored *The George Burns and Gracie Allen Show*.

Right: This vintage advertisement touted the fact that "You can make all your favorite cookies—*all of them*—from this one package—Nestlé Cookie Mix!"

22

The Right Recipe

Top: To address spoilage, Carnation Company founder E. A. Stuart automated his canning process in 1902. A century later, modern machinery continues to pack his first product. The Carnation Company grew from that single, signature offering to more than 200 products when Nestlé purchased the company in 1985.

Inset: Early 20th century stamps promoted Carnation Company's iconic Carnation Milk.

When Nestlé acquired Carnation in 1985, it shook the business world. At $3 billion, it was the largest non-oil acquisition in history at the time. Nestlé doubled in size overnight. Along with the classic Carnation brands, Nestlé added pet food brands Friskies® and Fancy Feast®. But in many ways, it was a long time coming.

Carnation had enjoyed a successful ride. It had increased earnings for 31 consecutive years, topping out at $194.8 million in earnings in 1983. An 18 percent return on investment was the industry's highest.

Beyond the cultural compatibility and long-term success, there were other reasons that Nestlé was interested in Carnation. "Of course, they're acquiring brands," said Joe Weller, former CEO of Nestlé USA. "But Nestlé looked at it a lot differently. They were really acquiring US leadership—that's what they really wanted. At the end of the day, the top 20 Carnation managers continued to manage the company, just like they did before the acquisition."

Libby's on the Label, Label, Label

THE FAMOUS PUMPKIN MAKER STARTED OUT PRODUCING PRODUCTS that could not be further from the key ingredient for a Thanksgiving pie.

Initially founded as Libby, McNeill & Libby (LM&L) in Chicago, Illinois in 1868, the first product was beef in brine—also known as corned beef. In 1875, the company was the first to begin mechanically compressing meat into cans. It produced its meat in trapezoid-shaped cans and transported real meat products to Chicago using refrigerated rail cars—both innovations at the time.

The corned beef product was an award winner, earning first place prizes at expositions. It also made it near the North Pole as part of sustenance for Admiral Robert Byrd's expedition in 1905.

By the early 1910s, LM&L found some measure of success with canned pineapple and shifted more of its resources into fruits and vegetables, with more than 100 products in all. Production expanded to California and Hawaii. By the beginning of World War I, Libby's had more than 3,000 canneries across the United States.

During the war, *Libby*'s meat products—and its key-open can—were included in emergency ration kits for US soldiers. In the 1920s and 1930s, the company expanded with international plants in Europe. After World War II, Libby's expanded into frozen foods.

But Libby's production of pumpkins made it enduring. In 1929, Libby's purchased Dickinson & Company, acquiring its pumpkin-packing plant in Illinois.

Nestlé purchased Libby's in 1976. Today, the Morton, Illinois plant grows and processes 85 percent of the world's canned pumpkins, using a proprietary seed.

In 1985, the purchase of Carnation and its Evaporated Milk by Nestlé brought the two key ingredients for pumpkin pie under one roof.

Above: Libby's easy pumpkin pie mix promotes the use of Carnation Milk.

Below left: In the 1950s, Libby's expanded into frozen food, but continued to advertise its popular canned pumpkin.

Below: A 1980s Libby's advertisement touted pumpkin cookies.

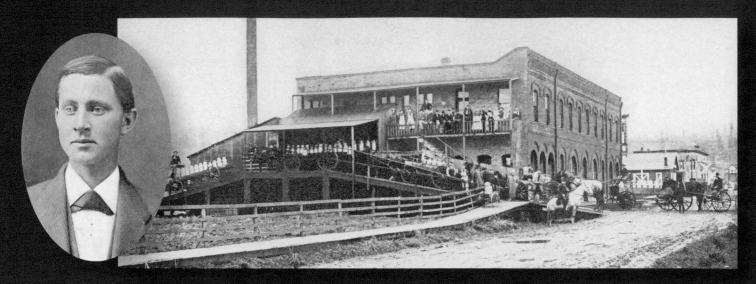

This page: Elbridge A. Stuart (inset) founded the Pacific Coast Condensed Milk Company (top) in 1899 with partner Tom Yerxa. Little did he realize it would evolve into the Carnation empire that Nestlé would acquire 80-plus years later.

Above: E. A. Stuart (middle) and Illinois Governor Frank O. Lowden pose with Segis Pietertje Prospect shortly after she established her World's Record production of 37,381.4 pounds of milk in 1920.

Carnation Milk: From Contented Cows

ONE CANNOT ACCUSE ELBRIDGE A. STUART OF LIVING A RISK-FREE life. The grocer founded the Pacific Coast Condensed Milk Company in 1899 with partner Tom Yerxa. How milk was converted from what the dairy farmers delivered each morning into a canned product was a process known only to one key employee and remained a mystery to both Stuart and Yerxa.

By 1901, the operation was deeply in debt, and Yerxa wanted out. Rather than fold the company, Stuart bought him out and expanded, purchasing a can-making machine.

"Two things were firmly in my mind," Stuart would later write. "One was supreme faith in the quality of my product. The other was that evaporated and sterilized milk—*Carnation* Milk as it is known in the markets of the country—would eventually be one of the largest single articles in the grocery business."

Stuart's belief was rewarded. In its first 75 years of operation, it failed to turn a profit only three times: 1901, 1920, and 1932.

A second plant opened in 1902 to make Sanipure milk for infants.

To help grow the business, Stuart had to start at the source: his own dairy farm. He brought in superior milking cattle from around the world and developed a breeding program. He sold cattle to local farmers who would sell milk back to him. He purchased a farm in 1908.

"He ended up expanding the property to about 1,600 acres eventually," said Bob Kosters, a retired *Nestlé* employee and part-time archivist. "When he started his program, the average cow in the United States would produce somewhere between 3,000 to 4,000 pounds of milk a year. By 1920, he had a cow here that produced over 37,000 pounds of milk in one year."

By 1919, Carnation and Helvetia Pure (later Pet) formed an overseas affiliate, the American Milk Condensing Company.

Carnation—Best Milk of All

By World War II, Carnation had expanded to include fresh dairy, ice cream, cereal, and pet food. Soon after, it had ventured into powdered milk and products for the manufacture of color photography. Cat food, instant breakfast drink, and dog biscuits followed in 1955.

By the 1970s, Carnation had expanded well beyond milk and related items into every type of food imaginable. Its Chef-mate® line served food professionals. Sandwich spreads made life easier for the home cook. Contadina® tomato products and instant potatoes were in the family, too.

When Nestlé acquired Carnation in 1985, Carnation had more than 200 products in its portfolio.

"Before companies like Carnation, if you wanted milk you had to have a cow. And you could never go very far away because that cow had to be milked twice a day. E. A. Stuart's process for evaporated milk (removing about 60% of the water and canning it) gave everyone access to the goodness and health benefits of milk."

—BOB KOSTERS
retired Nestlé employee
and archivist

CARNATION MILK (1944)

CONTADINA TOMATO PASTE (1965)

Left: Period advertising promoting some of Carnation Company's more iconic products in its diverse family.

A New Division

Baking is a relatively new division within Nestlé USA, focusing on *Libby's*, *Toll House*, and *Carnation* products. Breaking out the three was an opportunity to "drive these businesses for growth," said Hyder Raheem, vice president and general manager of the Baking Division. "In the past, we had really utilized these businesses as kind of a profit generator to feed other divisions because it is a fairly profitable division, but these brands had a latent equity that we weren't really leveraging, and if we could focus on it, we could drive growth."

It didn't hurt that the three brands have long, deep histories. But there needed to be an emphasis on how they are "relevant for the consumer today."

The consolidation also came at a time in which Nestlé was focusing on nutrition, health, and wellness. Consolidation comes with a realization that "every consumer is a bit different," said Paul Grimwood, chairman and CEO of Nestlé USA. "Every category is a bit different.

"You have to really understand the nuances of what the consumer wants when it comes to nutrition, health, and wellness in particular categories. So you look at indulgent categories. We're not taking out all of the ingredients that make our indulgent products so delicious. But we do want to give consumers healthier options, even when they're treating themselves. It is about being transparent, providing guidance, portion guidance, and responsible consumption."

Right: Nestlé Semi-Sweet chocolate formed the key ingredient for what became the quintessential chocolate chip cookie—the world-famous Nestlé Toll House cookie.

Below: Nestlé has products to help anyone bake up delectable goodies in their own kitchen, like the Famous Fudge baking kit, the Cookie Brownie kit, and the Pumpkin Bread kit.

Toll House: Baking the Very Best

RUTH WAKEFIELD WAS A DIETITIAN and food lecturer who purchased a Massachusetts inn with her husband. The Toll House Inn drew tourists from all around the world.

In the kitchen there, Wakefield created an American food staple. The lore differs slightly: Some legends have it that Wakefield was making chocolate cookies and ran out of baker's chocolate. Other tales say that she made a popular nut cookie and was looking to branch out.

Regardless of how Wakefield first put a chopped Nestlé semi-sweet bar [above] into batter, her invention—the Toll House® cookie—helped make Nestlé a household name in the United States.

Wakefield published her recipe in a second edition of her cookbook, *Ruth Wakefield's Toll-House Tried and True Recipes*, and the cookie took off. The cookies became so popular that Marjorie Husted (also known as Betty Crocker) invited Wakefield on her radio program.

Nestlé capitalized on the cookie relationship, purchasing rights to Wakefield's recipe for $1 and began printing the recipe on the bags of pre-chopped semi-sweet chocolate pieces, advertised as ready-to-use morsels for Toll House cookies.

Through the years, the Nestlé morsel line had expanded to include a number of options: butterscotch, mint, and spice. In 1994, *Nestlé* brought its baking brands together under the *Toll House* name, including refrigerated cookie dough, which was launched in 1993.

Above: During World War II, Nestlé urged families to send a taste of home to their soldiers overseas— featuring the Toll House cookie, of course.

Below: This commemorative tin celebrates 75 years of Toll House cookies.

1863

Mineral water from a French spring is bottled. Some years later, a local farmer acquires the Les Bouillens spring in Vergèze, France, and sets up a partnership that will eventually become Perrier. The then-obscure mineral water is initially bottled at this site.

1903

European aristocrat Sir St. John Harmsworth purchases property in France on which the Les Bouillens mineral springs reside. He renames the springs after the physician who introduced him to the magical sparkling waters, Dr. Perrier.

1985

Perrier introduces three new twists: orange-, lemon-, and lime-flavored mineral water.

1992

Nestlé acquires Source Perrier, based in Paris, parent company of The Perrier Group of America. Several years later, Nestlé rechristens the newly purchased group Nestlé Waters.

1999

Two other imported brands join the Nestlé Waters family: Acqua Panna, an Italian still water that traces its roots back centuries, and S.Pellegrino, an Italian sparkling water that eventually acquired the Acqua Panna brand.

2000

Nestlé Waters purchases Canadian company Aberfoyle, which supplied about half of Walmart's bottled water business. The brand eventually transitions to the future billion-dollar brand Nestlé Pure Life.

2013

The Andy Warhol Foundation teams up with Perrier to mark the brand's 150th anniversary by launching limited-edition pop art bottles and cans.

2015

Nestlé Pure Life starts The Ripple Effect Movement to encourage healthy beverage choices.

MAKING WATER POPULAR

WATER IS ABUNDANT ON THE EARTH AND IN HUMAN BODIES, accounting for 71 percent of the Earth's surface and about 60 percent of an adult body's makeup. With single-serve bottles of non-sparkling water widely available and a surge of interest in healthier alternatives, soft drinks' dominance as the drink of choice waned, helping drive the demand for bottled water.

Much of this change has been driven by Nestlé Waters North America Inc., which evolved from a company then called Great Waters of France that imported a popular French mineral water to one that became well known in supermarkets with 15 distinct beverage brands.

Opposite: In the 1880s, a local farmer acquired the Les Bouillens spring in Vergèze, France, and set up a partnership that led to the birth of Perrier Sparkling Natural Mineral Water. The mineral water is still bottled at this site.

Right: Perrier's familiar bottle design is easily recognized around the world. This bottle was in use from 1903 until about 1948.

Right: Workers bottle Perrier at the Vergèze, France factory in the 1930s. Decades later, the beverage became the drink of choice among many in the United States.

Below: Long before Perrier came to the United States, it transformed its look again. This distinctive small bottle was in use from 1948 until about 1990.

A French Import

The Perrier Group of America was founded to bring a long-established European brand—Perrier®—to the United States. The sparkling mineral water can trace its legendary roots back to some of Europe's leading warriors. Legend has it that Hannibal stopped at Les Bouillens mineral springs to refresh after defeating the Roman Army. Napoleon, it is said, allowed the development of the mineral springs.

But it was a prominent European aristocrat—Sir St. John Harmsworth—who built the enterprise. In 1903, Harmsworth purchased the property on which the mineral springs resided; he renamed them after the physician who had introduced him to the magical sparkling waters, Dr. Perrier. Harmsworth is credited with devising a *Perrier* signature: the distinct glass bottle shape, modeled after two wooden exercise clubs that he used after a leg injury.

Perrier was popular throughout Europe, but did not get expanded awareness and distribution in the United States until 1976, although it was distributed as early as 1904. In 1985, the company introduced three twists—orange-, lemon-, and lime-flavored mineral water.

Perrier laid the groundwork for a more sophisticated shift that was happening to the American palate, believes Jane Lazgin, director of corporate communications for Nestlé Waters North America Inc. "The advent of *Perrier* being more widely available to Americans in the late 1970s really made people think differently about water, particularly sparkling water," said

Lazgin, who was the ninth employee to join parent company Great Waters of France, Inc. in 1977. "*Perrier* was positioned as a calorie-free refreshment beverage instead of a sweetened drink or even alcohol. You would find it at the most current clubs and restaurants and bars in urban cities. And from there, it caught on."

It also arrived along with a health-conscious movement, which Perrier tapped into. "By then it had become available in grocery stores and gourmet stores. So the brand became much more widely known and available to people," Lazgin said.

"People were choosing a simple, delightful beverage with a French heritage that had no calories and nothing artificial. We knew, over time, that people would want healthier things to drink."

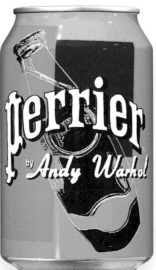

"Prior to 1990, most bottled water was consumed for tap water replacement, either in a five-gallon jug delivered to your home or a gallon or two-gallon jug that you picked up at the store. But when we put it in small plastic containers in late 1989, that was the first time somebody could walk into a convenience store and buy something other than a carbonated soft drink or a juice product."

— **KIM JEFFERY**
former Nestlé Waters CEO

This page: The Andy Warhol Foundation teamed up with Perrier to mark the brand's 150th anniversary by launching limited-edition pop art bottles and cans in 2013.

Nestlé Waters North America is Born

Nestlé acquired Perrier, then a $600 million company, in 1992. "They already had some water companies in Europe, but small ones, and this really put them on the map globally," said Kim Jeffery, Nestlé Waters former CEO, who joined Perrier in 1978.

With the acquisition, Nestlé stood poised to capitalize on a change that Perrier had helped introduce: the individual packaging that was common in other beverages, but had not yet been introduced to water.

"Prior to that, you had *Perrier* in small bottles, but they were glass bottles, and it was sparkling," Lazgin said. "Now water, simply refreshing water, was in the same kind of packages and available at the same kind of places you would find any other beverage. You wouldn't take one gallon of water into the movies or give it to a child during a soccer match or bring it with you to an airport or any situations where, today, those small, single-serve bottles are commonly chosen. That opened up a world of opportunity for people to make water part of their life. And it was easy to choose. They didn't have to examine labels. Didn't even really have to refrigerate it. It was in a resealable bottle. It was so simple and so convenient that people really started to choose water more and more, and particularly for their kids."

Nestlé formed Nestlé Waters France as a global business unit with the Perrier purchase. Nestlé Waters North America is the US-based company. The pieces had come together, and Nestlé was about to transform the world.

Bottled water first became popular in the United States when Perrier was imported from France. Perrier laid the initial groundwork for Nestlé Waters' changing the beverage preference of Americans.

Water from various Maine
springs is sourced by Nestlé
Waters for Roland Spring
brand natural spring water.
Here, Lower Range
Pond is pictured.

Top: The Poland Spring Bottling Plant and Spring House.

Above: Water was bottled on site, circa 1906–1970.

Tapping Regional Springs

NOT CONTENT TO JUST OFFER THE FRENCH IMPORT, THE PERRIER Group of America purchased a number of small regional brands to build out its portfolio. Nestlé purchased the group in 1992 and eventually renamed it Nestlé Waters North America.

America has a bounty of natural springs, some of which were used as sources for spring water, bottled more than a century ago as a source of clean, fresh water. Perrier Group had purchased brands such as Arrowhead®, Deer Park®, Ice Mountain®, Poland Spring®, and Zephyrhills®. Each had a long legacy in its respective region, and all continue to be strong regional players.

The *Arrowhead* brand grew from a cold water spring in the San Bernardino Mountains of California. A giant rock formation shaped like an arrowhead points to the springs. In 1889, a hotel was built on the site, with guests raving about the water, prompting a bottling operation to be set up in the hotel's basement. By 1905, water was being shipped to Los Angeles. Today *Arrowhead* Brand Mountain Spring Water is sourced from mountain springs in California, Colorado, and British Columbia.

The *Deer Park* brand also had its start with a hotel that catered to those seeking what they believed to be the healing properties of natural springs, this one in the Appalachian Mountains of western Maryland. The Baltimore & Ohio Railroad noted the benefits of the waters and bottled it for its train passengers in 1873. Today *Deer Park* Natural Spring water comes from carefully selected natural springs located in several states.

Ozarka® Brand Natural Spring Water got its start in Eureka, Arkansas. In 1905, the Ozarka Spring Water Company began bottling the "healing waters" of the springs and delivering it in glass-lined rail cars. Today *Ozarka* Brand Spring Water comes from Roher Spring, Piney Woods Springs, and Moffitt Spring in Texas. It is no longer from Eureka Springs.

The *Poland Spring* brand grew from a Maine spring that was purported to have healing properties. It too gave birth to a hotel where guests, including celebrities and notable politicians, would come to play golf and enjoy the outdoors. It was first bottled in 1845 and quickly became an award winner, earning the Medal of Excellence at the World's Columbian Exhibition in 1893 and named "the best spring water in the country" at the St. Louis World's Fair in 1904. Although that spring is no longer in use, its heritage is celebrated at the Poland Spring Museum and *Poland Spring* brand. *Poland Spring* brand comes from several carefully selected spring sources located in Maine.

The town of Zephyrhills, Florida, was born in 1909 when it was selected as a colony for Civil War veterans, thanks in part to its abundant sources of good water. It was first bottled in 1964. Today *Zephyrhills* Natural Spring Water comes from several natural springs located throughout the state.

Two other imported brands would later join the Nestlé Waters family: Acqua Panna®, an Italian still water that traces its roots back centuries, and S.Pellegrino, an Italian sparkling mineral water that eventually acquired Acqua Panna. Both became part of Nestlé in 1999.

Nestlé Waters North America bottling facilities: the Arrowhead facility, Los Angeles (top); the Deer Park, Pennsylvania facility (middle); and the Zephyrhills, Florida facility (bottom).

HEALTHY HYDRATION

Nestlé Waters North America Inc. has the components to capitalize on—if not drive—a change in Americans' preference. The quest for a healthy lifestyle is beginning to edge sugary soft drinks out of the picture. Water has become the go-to beverage. Nestlé Waters has joined a national movement, launching its Healthy Hydration campaign.

But the growth in bottled water is coming at a time when environmental issues are increasingly a concern, with droughts plaguing some water resources, and a challenge arising about plastic waste.

Opposite: With natural spring, mineral, and purified drinking waters in its portfolio, Nestlé Waters is single-handedly changing consumers' beverage patterns.

Right: In November 2015, Nestlé Pure Life brand started The Ripple Effect Movement to encourage healthy beverage choices.

Nestlé® Pure Life®
Purified Water

With the regional spring and mineral water brands in its portfolio, Nestlé had another opportunity when the Canadian company Aberfoyle was sold. Aberfoyle had something of extreme value: about half of Walmart's bottled water business.

"I went up to Canada and negotiated with the family," said Kim Jeffery, then-CEO of Nestlé Waters. "It was a time when the Canadian dollar was worth about 70 cents to the US dollar. I didn't know what to do with that brand, and I went to Walmart and said, 'Look, would you guys care if we sort of massaged the brand and it became *Nestlé Pure Life* over a couple-year period with a soft conversion of labeling over that time period?'"

Nestlé Pure Life brand was already in use globally—primarily in developing nations. "I think we need a brand like that in the United States because Coke and Pepsi have Dasani® and Aquafina®," Jeffery said. One national Nestlé Waters brand would allow for more efficient operations throughout the United States. "We converted the label over in about 18 months, and we used Walmart as our foundation, and *Nestlé Pure Life* is a billion-dollar brand today," Jeffery said.

The growth of the category meant a lot of work in between, however. Nestlé Waters launched a massive building program, adding 14 plants between 2000 and 2011, Jeffery said. "It just was like a runaway train."

The missio
Leadership in
Green Buildin

But the gre
Between 1994
water bottles

"You want t
consumer doe
were launchin
of polyester o
waste anywhe

That mean
process that b
saving on the
point, we were
to be good for
ribs [in the bo
then the ques
need?' And so
be, and we car
eliminating th
and reduce pla

ReadyRefresh by Nestlé is a customizable beverage delivery service. Customers can choose to have more than just water delivered directly to their home or office.

5

We have ni...
manageme...

1. Creating

A zero water facto...
raw materials and...
for groundwater or...

2. Reducing

We use 'Water Targ...
opportunities to fu...
as the technology v...
helped us identify v...
in 80 of our factorie...

3. Recycling

Recycling wastewat...
factories is one eff...

At some Nestlé Wat...
California, changes...

4. Implemen...

The Alliance for Wate...
international standa...
managing water in a...
socially, and econom...

We will implement th...
factories in Californi...

5. Working i...

We support collective...
scarcity, working tog...
bodies and other stal...
and global water issu...

We are a founding sig...
Compact CEO Water...
develop, implement a...
sustainability policies...

These effo...
144 n...
more inform...
water...

Local Springs Provide High-Quality Water

Hoffman Spring (above) is located in New Tripoli, Pennsylvania. Other Nestlé spring sources in the state include Greenwaltz Springs, Sasoonan Springs, Arrowhead Springs, Pine Grove Springs, and Valley View Springs.

BOTTLING ITS WATER CLOSE TO THE MARKETPLACE HAS A POSITIVE environmental benefit, too. On average, Nestlé Waters' products travel less than 300 miles from source to the shelf, reducing fuel use and emissions.

Tim Brown, CEO of Nestlé Waters, found consumers were in favor of the change to lighter weight bottles. "There is something refreshing about water, and with this plastic being quite thin, you can feel the condensation on the outside," he said. "It just makes you even more happy about refreshing yourself."

The environmental efforts also have been important to the culture at Nestlé Waters. "We are a natural resource company," said Jane Lazgin, director of corporate communications for Nestlé Waters. "We can go to Maine or go to California or go anywhere where we have springs and tromp out in the woods to these beautiful, unhurried, serene places. So we've always had great awe and respect for the environment. That fuels our desire to be responsible and attract employees who are environmentally conscious people. Bottled water is enjoying this great popularity among consumers, but there's also a benefit to the environment and to sustainability, because bottled water uses less water and less plastic than any other packaged beverage."

Healthy Hydration

Nestlé Waters has been able to ride a crest of the goal to live a healthy lifestyle. In 2013, the company joined the Drink Up Intitiative, a part of the Partnership for a Healthier America.

The Drink Up campaign was just one segment of Nestlé Waters' healthy hydration initiative. The company is a strategic partner of the US Department of Agriculture Center for Nutrition Policy and Promotion, whose mission is to improve the health of Americans by developing and promoting dietary guidance that links scientific research to the nutrition needs of consumers. Nestlé Waters worked with more than 200,000 students on a "Healthy Steps for Healthy Lives®" campaign to encourage good habits for eating, drinking, and staying active.

"We've single-handedly changed consumers' beverage patterns," Jeffery said. "About 70 percent of the industry's growth has come directly out of carbonated soft drinks. Per capita consumption of carbonated soft drinks is down 25 percent in the last 12 years, and the decline in caloric intake from carbonated beverages is huge. I really think it's changing beverage consumption in America."

In the coming years, bottled water will surpass carbonated soft drinks as the most popular beverage, a "dramatic shift in preferences among consumers," Lazgin said. "It is people really thinking about what they're drinking, what they're giving to their children. But Perrier® in that little green bottle with its sparkle from France changed everything."

Above: The first-of-its-kind Drink Up initiative program is aimed at encouraging and inspiring everyone to drink more water.

Below left: Nestlé Waters offers a wide variety of refreshing beverages delivered right to customers' doors.

Below right: Healthy hydration is important for everyone, no matter their activity level.

Nestlé

1938

Researchers in Nestlé Swiss laboratories create the first nonperishable coffee. Their innovative product—the world's first instant coffee—makes its way to the United States as Nescafé the following year.

1943

Nestlé opens two American production facilities to keep up with the growing demand for Nescafé. The military supplies the popular instant coffee to US troops during World War II.

1948

Nestlé launches Quik Chocolate Powder, allowing parents all over the United States to make their children a quick glass of chocolate milk. Nestlé also debuts its Nestea brand so consumers can make iced tea by stirring Nestea crystals into cold water.

1960s

Nestlé debuts its Taster's Choice brand, adding to consumers' options among instant coffee brands.

1985

Nestlé buys Carnation
Company and its popular
non-dairy creamer,
Coffee-mate.

1985

Nestlé adds two coffee
companies—Hills Bros.
Company and MJB—to
its impressive roster,
further solidifying Nestlé's
presence in the American
coffee market.

2009

Nestlé opens a LEED-certified,
state-of-the-art facility to
manufacture Coffee-mate,
Nesquik, and other products
in Anderson, Indiana.

2015

Nestlé pledges to reduce
added sugar in its Nesquik
product, and removes
all artificial colors and flavors
from powdered Nesquik
as part of the company's
commitment to nutrition,
health, and wellness.

Nescafé takes choice coffee beans to blend, roast, and grind. Then they are percolated to produce a rich aroma and smooth taste that is captured through the company's innovative spray-dry or freeze-dry process.

How Instant Coffee is Made

EVER SINCE *Nescafé* HIT THE MARKET, THERE HAVE BEEN DOZENS OF theories attempting to explain how instant coffee is made. Even back in 1957, Nestlé reported that there were people who believed "that instant coffee is nothing more than ground coffee pulverized to a fine powder—such a method, of course, would produce only a muddy, undrinkable potion when boiling water was added."

The reality is that Nestlé's innovative process is actually quite simple. "*Nescafé* soluble coffee is made from 100 percent natural coffee beans, just like any other coffee," Nestlé says on its website. "Nothing artificial is added or used." Nestlé blends, roasts, and grinds the beans and then percolates them. "After percolation, the brewed coffee is either spray-dried or freeze-dried," Nestlé noted. During spray drying, the coffee passes through a spray nozzle into hot air, atomizing the coffee into small particles. Those are then moistened and dried one more time to create the *Nescafé* product you see.

If the process involves freeze drying, Nestlé snap freezes the coffee at -40 degrees Celsius and grinds the coffee down to the appropriate granule size. Nestlé subsequently applies heat to evaporate the ice crystals, and the freeze-dried coffee is then packaged into jars for products such as *Nescafé*.

Beyond Java

Even before Nestlé debuted its groundbreaking *Nescafé* product in 1938, a Swiss chemist named George Wander was studying the nutritional profile of barley malt. In 1904, Wander combined the barley with other well-known ingredients, including milk, egg, and cocoa, to create the classic nutritional drink *Ovaltine*, which Nestlé acquired in the United States as part of the Novartis acquisition in 2007.

In 1948, Nestlé launched its Quik Chocolate Powder, allowing parents all over the United States to make their children a quick glass of chocolate milk. A few years later, the strawberry flavor of Quik hit the shelves, providing a second popular option for the instant beverage. The name changed from Quik to Nesquik® in the 1990s, by which time it was available as both a powder and a ready-to-drink beverage in bottles.

The same year that Quik joined the American lexicon, Nestlé also debuted its Nestea® brand, which allowed consumers to make iced tea by stirring *Nestea* crystals into cold water. "A real innovation, *Nestea* is the only powdered tea with the instant dissolving feature," Nestlé announced in June 1956. The company noted that the product saved the work of making iced tea and featured "the complete absence of tea bags and the mess that accompanies them."

This page
Carnation
supermar

Opposite:
Nesquik b
outside th
very visib

Amazing!

First second—
cold milk

—next second
stir in Quik

and you get
RICH CHOCOLATY
MILK...M-M-M

—instantly with
NESTLÉ'S
Quik!

...the fastest you ever
mixed—the best you ever
tasted! Because this amazing
new Quik mixes with cold milk—
INSTANTLY! No beating...no
bother...and no refrigerating!
Just stir and serve!
P.S.—It stays chocolaty
all the way through!

WITH THAT FAMOUS NESTLÉ'S CHOCOLATE FLAVOR

Nestlé Invests in the US

In 2009, Nestlé opened a LEED-certified, state-of-the-art facility to manufacture *Coffee-mate*, *Nesquik*, and other products in Anderson, Indiana. LEED stands for Leadership in Energy and Environmental Design. These structures are built using more environmentally conscientious construction materials and techniques.

The Anderson facility employs more than 700 people and represents the largest capital investment Nestlé has made in the United States since acquiring the Carnation Company in 1985.

Covering over a million square feet, the production area is among the largest Nestlé has in the United States and produces up to four million bottles of product every day. The Nestlé Anderson facility produces aseptic (shelf-stable) beverages for some of America's most favorite brands, including *Nesquik* ready-to-drink, *Nestlé Coffee-mate* liquid, and BOOST® nutritional drinks.

Left: Nestlé launched Quik in 1948, touting the ease with which one could make a quick glass of chocolate milk.

Below: This photo shows the impressive size of Nestle's facility in Anderson, Indiana (below). When it opened in 2009, the facility covered 880,000 square feet. After two expansions (next page), the facility has grown to the equivalent of 23 football fields, or 1.3 million square feet.

"Consumers' expectations of foods and beverages are evolving towards purity and new health. We've earned our consumers' vote by leading in great taste and nutrition improvements. Our commitment for 2016 and beyond continues to address these forward-looking trends by expanding the number of all natural and new health choices across our most popular brands."

—ALICIA ENCISO
President of the
Nestlé USA Beverage Division

Looking Ahead

Nestlé continues to focus on providing refreshing, healthy beverages to people everywhere while keeping an eye on sustainability. The company has ardently worked to buy sustainable coffee and provide technical help to coffee farmers all over the world while ensuring that the manufacturing processes are energy efficient and that the company uses responsible packaging.

In 2015, Nestlé pledged to reduce added sugar in its *Nesquik* products and removed all artificial colors and flavors from powdered *Nesquik* as part of the company's commitment to nutrition, health, and wellness. "Given our market leadership, *Nesquik* and *Coffee-mate* Natural Bliss® have created even more nutritious and great-tasting options for our consumers," said Rob Case, former president of the Nestlé USA Beverage Division. "Guided by Nestlé's strict nutrition criteria as well as consumer desires, we've begun this journey by reducing sugar across our Nesquik portfolio. *Coffee-mate Natural Bliss* provides better nutrition, health, and wellness as an all-natural coffee creamer made with no genetically engineered ingredients and real milk and cream from cows not treated with added growth hormone."

Above: Nestlé has cut the sugar content in its popular Nesquik drinks, reducing the amount of sugar by 45 percent overall.

Left: Coffee-mate is available as both powder and liquid, and in reduced fat and sugar-free varieties as well.

Nestlé

1986

Nespresso SA, a Nestlé Group company, is founded. Inspired by Luigi Bezzera's original espresso coffee concept, the company develops a revolutionary system of portioned, encapsulated coffee and dedicated machines to deliver perfect coffee.

1989

After testing the concept in Switzerland, Japan, and Italy, the Nespresso system is introduced in Switzerland.

2003

Designed to promote production and supply of sustainable, highest quality coffee, the Nespresso AAA Sustainable Quality Program is launched, in collaboration with the non-government organization The Rainforest Alliance.

2006

Nespresso opens its first North American boutique bar in Manhattan, located on Madison Avenue.

2013

Nespresso unites worldwide sustainability experts to create the Nespresso Sustainability Advisory Board. The company sources 84% of its coffee from the Nespresso AAA Sustainable Quality™ Program and reduces the carbon footprint of a cup of Nespresso by 20%, reaching commitments made in 2009.

2014

Catering to North American tastes, Nespresso debuts the VertuoLine. This revolutionizes the coffee experience by delivering an 8 ounce cup of coffee with crema, along with traditional espressos.

2015

Nespresso adds to the VertuoLine product range, debuting the Evoluo Machine, capable of brewing both large-cup coffees and espresso, making it customizable to the coffee drinker's preference.

2015

Within a month after launching, Evoluo is selected by *O Magazine* to join the latest list of Oprah Winfrey's "Favorite Things" for 2015.

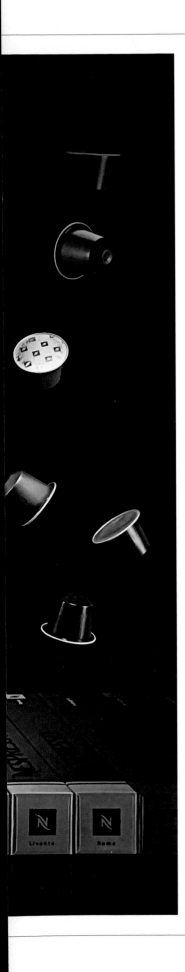

A NEW WAY TO DRINK COFFEE

MUCH LIKE NESTLÉ ITSELF, NESPRESSO® HAS ITS ROOTS IN EUROPE, but its innovative approach to making coffee was strongly in demand in the United States, prompting a *Nespresso©* revolution when it arrived stateside. Even the Nestlé executives could not have foreseen the exploding demand that the innovative coffee machine and its accompanying Grand Cru capsules and crema would have on the US population.

"Our capsules hold years of innovation, passion, and expertise ... a series of quality decisions which determine a unique aromatic and sensory profile for each Grand Cru."

—JAMES PERGOLA
Coffee Ambassador for Nespresso

The rich tastes and differing notes of Nespresso's OriginalLine (opposite) offer discerning coffee consumers a distinctive range of extraordinary Grand Cru coffees, each of them finished with Nespresso's signature crema (above right).

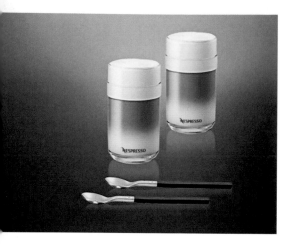

In addition to coffee makers and capsules, Nespresso offers accessories such as these elegant latte glasses designed for large-cup recipes, created especially for Nespresso's VertuoLine machines by designer Konstantin Grcic.

A 30-Year Tradition

Back in the late 1980s, most Americans considered espresso to be an exotic beverage enjoyed only by Europeans—and that was largely true, since many US cafés didn't serve the concentrated coffee at the time. However, Nestlé aimed to capitalize on the global popularity of espresso when the company launched its *Nespresso* concept. When the single-serve gourmet coffee machine debuted, it allowed consumers to serve barista-level coffees from the comfort of their homes.

Nespresso initially introduced two machines and four Grand Cru coffee varieties in Switzerland, and the concept quickly spread throughout the European continent. As with most gastronomic delights, Americans were eager to get their hands on the latest European sensation, and *Nespresso* machines began appearing on American countertops. Though *Nespresso* was an exotic novelty, the fact remained that it wasn't completely practical for most Americans, who preferred their coffee in large mugs rather than small espresso cups. "North Americans are different consumers," said Nestlé CEO Paul Bulcke. "They do drink espresso, but for special moments in high-level restaurants."

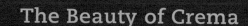

The Beauty of Crema

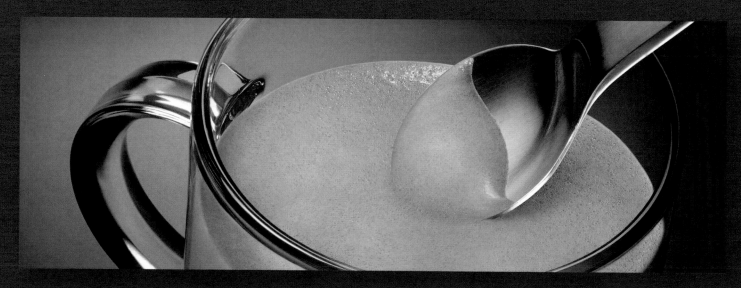

Smooth, creamy, exquisite. Crema is a naturally formed foam of coffee and air that preserves coffee aromas, enhances taste, and signifies world-class coffee.

IN ADDITION TO ITS SINGLE SERVE INNOVATION, NESPRESSO IS FAMOUS FOR the "crema" produced at the top of the coffee, which is created in the machine thanks to the combination of the water pressure, temperature, coffee quality, freshness, and coffee grinding. This creamy textured topping not only gives Nespresso coffee its distinctive appearance and flavor, but also serves to seal the aromas into the cup of coffee.

Filling American Coffee Mugs

To cater more astutely to American tastes, Nespresso debuted the VertuoLine of machines and capsules in 2014, which filled a larger cup of coffee. "We really believe our last year's growth in the United States was very solid, but we were limited to premium espresso coffees," Jean-Marc Duvoisin, CEO of Nespresso, told CNBC in a TV interview in 2014. "Now we are launching this new technology which will be able to deliver a large cup of very premium coffee."

"VertuoLine was positioned as a game-changer for the United States," said Nespresso Vice President of Customer Experience Barbara Jacobsen LaRocca. "We were introducing a better tasting cup of coffee using our capsule system. No longer would we need to advise customers how to make a "big" cup with the OriginalLine machine, using two-plus capsules! Now, we have a machine that makes a great iced coffee (my favorite) or a perfectly American-sized hot mug. Plus, with the introduction of flavored coffee offered as an everyday blend from day one—the expectations were high that the VertuoLine would be a success for the United States. The launch itself was very exciting! It was a true 360 touch point strategy, a new innovation launched only in North America, and the teams could not have been more proud to take part in this coffee revolution," said LaRocca.

Within a year after the VertuoLine launch in the United States, sales exceeded expectations. The growth prompted Nespresso to add a new, $308 million production facility to manufacture capsules specifically for the US market. By September 2015, American sales saw growth in the impressive double digits, compared to single-digit increases in Europe. "The United States expansion is going very well," Nespresso Chairman Patrice Bula told *Bloomberg News* at the time. "We have the growth we planned to have in Europe."

Above: A world-class team of Nespresso engineers and designers created the most intelligent, elegant, and ergonomic single-serve coffee system on the market today— VertuoLine.

Below: VertuoLine's proprietary extraction process provides a high level of precision as the machine recognizes—through barcode technology printed around the lip of the capsule— each expertly designed Grand Cru and adjusts the extraction parameters to brew each blend in the most optimal way.

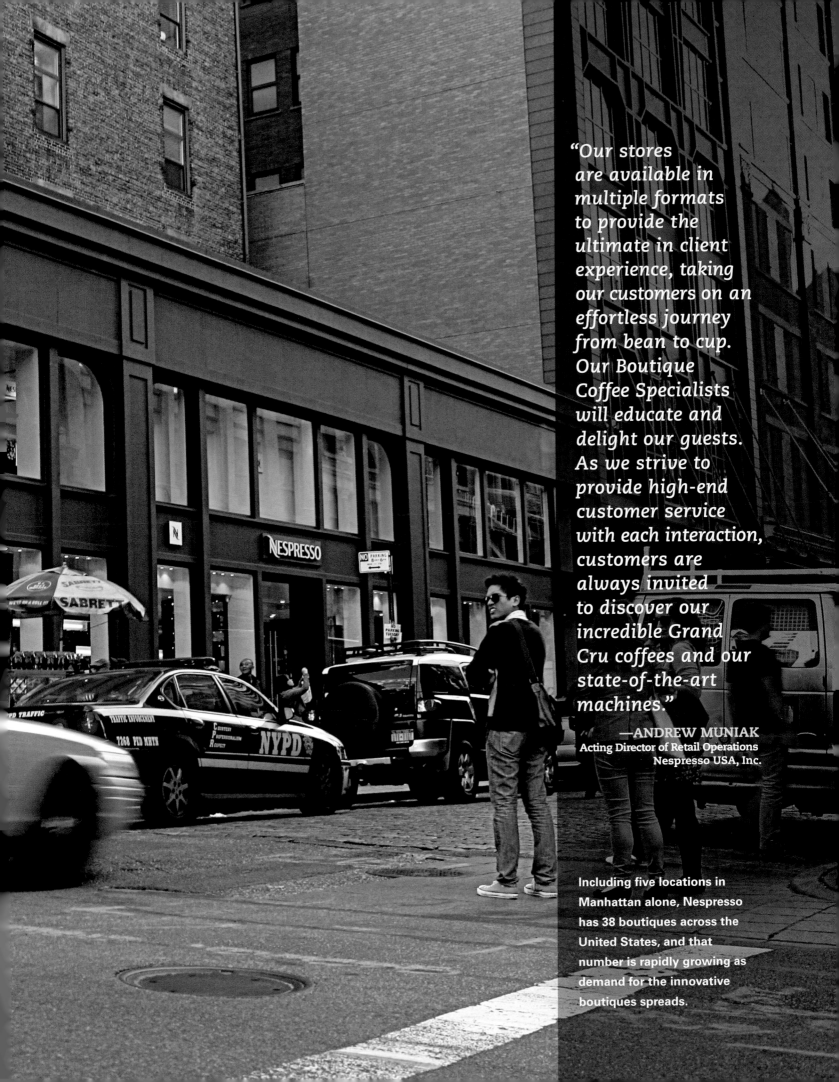

"Our stores are available in multiple formats to provide the ultimate in client experience, taking our customers on an effortless journey from bean to cup. Our Boutique Coffee Specialists will educate and delight our guests. As we strive to provide high-end customer service with each interaction, customers are always invited to discover our incredible Grand Cru coffees and our state-of-the-art machines."

—ANDREW MUNIAK
Acting Director of Retail Operations
Nespresso USA, Inc.

Including five locations in Manhattan alone, Nespresso has 38 boutiques across the United States, and that number is rapidly growing as demand for the innovative boutiques spreads.

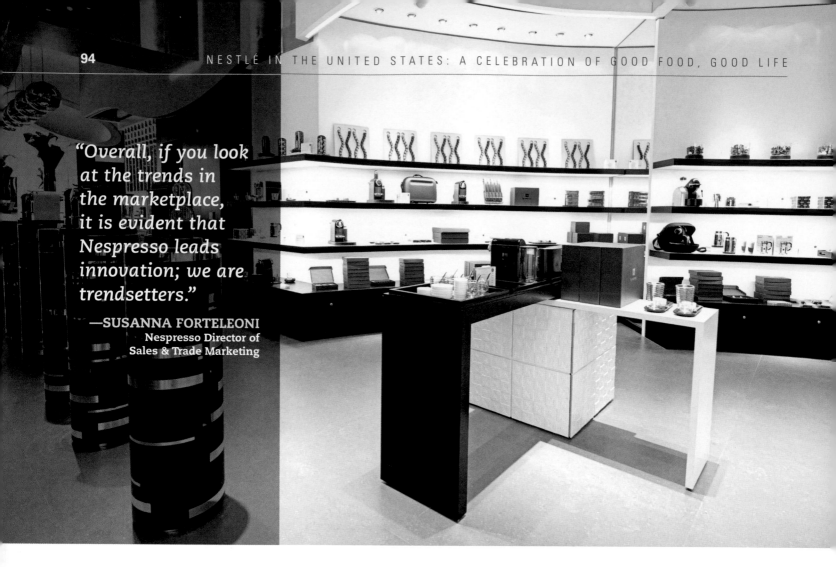

"*Overall, if you look at the trends in the marketplace, it is evident that Nespresso leads innovation; we are trendsetters.*"

—SUSANNA FORTELEONI
Nespresso Director of Sales & Trade Marketing

Nespresso boutiques (above) offer customers the opportunity to experience and purchase Nespresso's extensive selection of Espresso machines and Grand Cru coffees. Coffee specialists are on staff to offer demonstrations of the single-serve, easy-to-use Nespresso machines as well as guide customers through each unique profile of the Grand Cru selections available (below).

Nurturing the Consumer Connection

Nespresso is unique in that the company sells its coffee capsules solely on a direct-to-consumer basis (online, in *Nespresso* boutiques, and via phone), and that decision was part of an overall strategy to provide a distinctive experience for consumers. Nespresso is able to adjust and tweak its offerings because the company interacts with its Nespresso club members every time they order more capsules. This business model has allowed Nespresso to stay on the pulse of its community.

"If you don't have the direct connection, you can't ask consumers [what they think] and you don't have insight," Duvoisin told *The Wall Street Journal*. "It's very easy to go out and sell machines, but we don't sell machines; we sell coffee. If you're not sure that the machines are bought by people who want to drink good coffee every day, then you are fooling yourself. You have big sales of machines, people buy coffee at the beginning and then they taste it once or twice and then they stop. That's the worst thing you can do. So you should make sure the people who buy your machines are entering a pattern of ongoing coffee consumption."

Another way the company keeps in close touch with its customers is via the Nespresso boutiques. As of early 2016, there are 38 boutique locations throughout the United States that sell the company's namesake coffees. Consumers are able to taste-test new blends and check out the latest Nespresso coffee-making innovations. New locations will be added in 2016 and 2017.

Looking Ahead

Because the VertuoLine has proven so popular in the United States, Nespresso added to the product range, debuting the Evoluo machine in 2015. Evoluo can brew both large-cup coffees and espresso, making it customizable to the coffee drinker's preference. Within a month after launching, the new product had been selected by *O Magazine* to join the latest list of Oprah Winfrey's "Favorite Things" for 2015.

Nespresso has pledged to achieve its sustainability goals by 2020. The chief objective is to use 100 percent sustainably sourced coffee and 100 percent sustainably managed aluminum in its capsules by then, as well as becoming completely carbon-neutral. "Our sustainability approach has always been designed to do more than simply minimize impacts," Duvoisin said. "The development of even more innovative programs with our partners demonstrates our commitment to creating shared value and generating positive impacts for all stakeholders across the entire value chain."

"We're constantly trying to stand out and to prove that we are the best in terms of not only the product but the service that we deliver, and we're constantly challenging ourselves to wow the customer."

—KATERINA KAKANAS
Nespresso Customer Relations
Center Site Manager

The Evoluo machine, which expands the VertuoLine machine range and features an updated style, has the ability to produce both single-serve large-cup coffee *and* authentic espresso.

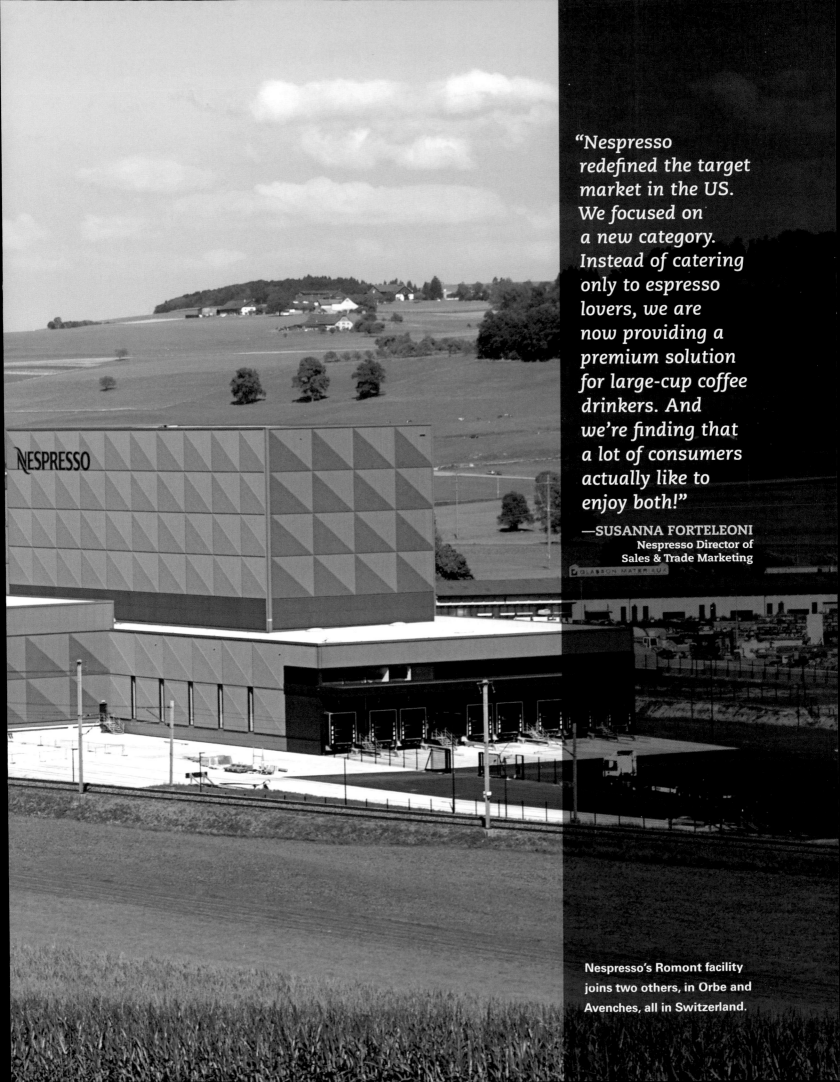

"Nespresso redefined the target market in the US. We focused on a new category. Instead of catering only to espresso lovers, we are now providing a premium solution for large-cup coffee drinkers. And we're finding that a lot of consumers actually like to enjoy both!"

—SUSANNA FORTELEONI
Nespresso Director of
Sales & Trade Marketing

Nespresso's Romont facility joins two others, in Orbe and Avenches, all in Switzerland.

Nestlé

DELUXE DOG CRATE

1894

In St. Louis, William H. Danforth and his partners, George Robinson and Will Andrews, sell a new animal feed made of corn, oats, and molasses mixed using shovels and packaged in 175-pound sacks.

1898

Danforth creates a line of breakfast cereals, including Ralston Barley Food and Hominy Grits. Health guru "Dr. Ralston," with 800,000 followers, endorses the products. Danforth's animal feed is named "Purina" to match the company's tagline, "Where Purity is Paramount."

1902

The company's name is changed from the Robinson-Danforth Commission Company to Ralston Purina.

1957

Ralston Purina becomes the first company to use a manufacturing process called extrusion to make dry dog food pieces that are uniform in size and appearance.

1962

Cat Chow debuts and quickly becomes the country's best-selling dry cat food.

1987

Purina debuts super-premium lines of dog food, including Pro Plan and Purina ONE.

2001

DECEMBER 11
Nestlé acquires Ralston Purina and will move its own pet care unit to St. Louis to be managed by the newly created Nestlé Purina PetCare Company.

2015

DECEMBER
Nestlé Purina US achieves an impressive 12 straight years of improved sales growth and profit, with $7.3 billion in sales.

OFFERING THE BEST FOR PETS

I N 1894, AMERICANS HAD BIGGER CONCERNS THAN WHAT TO FEED THEIR FARM animals. The country was in the throes of a financial panic that resulted in a weak dollar. The panic lasted until 1897, causing 15,000 businesses to go bankrupt and 500 banks to fail. This fact might have discouraged many typical entrepreneurs of the day from starting a business, but William H. Danforth was not typical.

In 1894, Danforth and his partners, George Robinson and Will Andrews, sold a new animal feed made of corn, oats, and molasses mixed using shovels and packaged in 175-pound sacks. The trio sold the product out of a St. Louis storefront, and by 1902 had named it "Purina®" to match the company's tagline, "Where Purity is Paramount." They adopted the signature checkerboard motif still seen in the company's packaging to this day.

By 1898, the economy bounced back, allowing Danforth to create a line of whole wheat *Purina* breakfast cereals. A popular health guru known as "Dr. Ralston" promptly endorsed the products, and 800,000 followers paid attention to his advice. Just four years later, the products were selling so quickly that the entire company changed its name to Ralston Purina. As a result of Dr. Ralston's influence, the company created new products, including Ralston Barley Food and Hominy Grits.

Opposite: A healthy pet will have bright eyes, a shiny coat, and playful personality. Purina pet food provides the nutrition pets need for a happy life.

Right: In the early 1900s, Purina feed bags featured company mascot Maud the mule.

Above: In 1926, Purina created its pet nutrition and care center in Missouri to study the best foods for pets.

Above right: An "L. L. Canine" Purina feed store in Illinois, circa 1922.

Below: Purina doesn't focus just on dogs—in 1962, the company launched its Cat Chow product.

The Debut of Chow

While Danforth was in France during World War I, he picked up on soldiers' use of the word "chow" to describe their meals. When he returned stateside, he began using the name "Chows" for his products. Whereas Danforth had a strong sense of what animals needed, his son Donald focused on researching what would be the healthiest options for them to thrive. In 1926, Purina created its first facility solely dedicated to studying the nutritional needs of companion animals.

That research wouldn't take long to pay off. In 1957, Purina became the first company to use a manufacturing process called extrusion to make dry dog food pieces that were uniform in size and appearance and that dogs absolutely loved.

Keith M. Schopp, vice president, corporate public relations, Nestlé Purina PetCare Company, North America, related the impact that the new process had on the pet food market:

> "Dog Chow® had already been around for quite a while, but this was a major innovation. It was a new, pressure-cooked, extruded *Dog Chow* formula that helped catapult Purina from an also-ran into a leader in the pet food business. That, coupled with the decision to sell the product in grocery stores, really tipped the scales."

The new *Purina Dog Chow* was so popular that Purina had to ration it to ensure that everyone who wanted to buy it got some. The company debuted Cat Chow® in 1962, which quickly became the country's best-selling dry cat food.

P.H.SPROAT Co.
DISTRIBUTORS

PURINA CHICKEN CHOWDER

MORE EGGS or money back — PURINA CHICKEN CHOWDER

MORE EGGS or money back PURINA CHICKEN CHOWDER

MORE MILK PURINA COW CHOW

HEALTH BABY CHICKS CHICKEN CHOWDER

MAUD'S NOSE KNOWS

IT'S O-MOLENE

PURINA CHICKEN CHOWDER

PURINA HEN CHOW

P. CHICKEN CHOWDER

Attention!!
Pigeon Owners —

WE SELL THE ONLY regularly Prepared Pigeon Feed
COME AND SEE IT

PURINA CHOWS
HORSES-COWS
POULTRY-HOGS
CHECKERBOARD BAGS

Purina offered nutritional food for many farm animals for years. Among the products pictured here are Pigeon Chow, Hen Chow, Chicken Chowder, Horse Chow, and Cow Chow.

New dog food discovery makes dogs eager eaters. It's a full course dog dinner complete with <u>real</u> meat meal. Just moisten and serve.

New Purina Dog Chow

> *"One of the best things that ever happened to Carnation was Nestlé, but one of the best things that ever happened to Nestlé was Purina."*
>
> **—JOHN VELLA**
> **Senior Vice President,**
> **Head of Global Strategic Business Unit**
> **and Research & Development**

A HEALTHIER HEAD START FOR FARM DOGS

Purina Dog Chow gives dogs a well-balanced ration table scraps can't match

It's true most dogs go for table scraps. But scrap feeding often amounts to "lick and a promise" feeding. Most times table scraps don't deliver the total nutrition that means a rugged, healthier dog.

That's why you ought to give your dog a head start on good health. Rely on a prepared food, same as you do for livestock and poultry. Purina animal nutritionists, who bring you the other Purina Chows

you know and trust, have come up with just the right dog food, a scientifically produced daily ration that gives dogs the nutrients they need for growth and rugged good health. And dogs relish Purina's Eager Eater flavor.

You ought to try Purina Dog Chow for your dog. At Purina Dealers and grocers in five thrifty sizes.

It takes a puppy a full year to outgrow Purina Puppy Chow.

Just because a puppy looks full grown, it doesn't mean he is. Our six-month-old Sheepdog is about six times the size he was at one month.

At nine or ten months, when he's about as big as he'll get on the outside, his bones and muscles are still developing, inside.

That's why a puppy needs the kind of extra nutrition he gets in Purina®Puppy

Chow®puppy food. For a full year, till he's full grown.

Make his first year one to grow on, with regular trips to the vet, and Purina Puppy Chow every day.

For a full year till he's full grown.

Nourishment so complete ...all you add is love.

PURINA DOG CHOW

This page and opposite: Purina Dog Chow ads as seen through the years. Nutrition is the common theme in all of the advertisements since it has always been the primary focus.

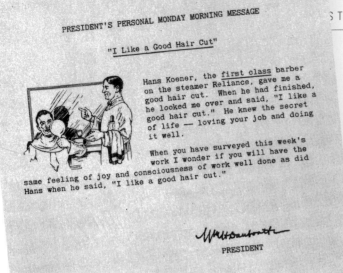

PRESIDENT'S PERSONAL MONDAY MORNING MESSAGE

"I Like a Good Hair Cut"

Hans Koener, the first class barber on the steamer Reliance, gave me a good hair cut. When he had finished, he looked me over and said, "I like a good hair cut." He knew the secret of life — loving your job and doing it well.

When you have surveyed this week's work I wonder if you will have the same feeling of joy and consciousness of work well done as did Hans when he said, "I like a good hair cut."

PRESIDENT

Oct. 7th 1929

Above: An example of one of William H. Danforth's Monday Morning Messages used to unite and inspire employees.

Bottom: Ralston Purina founder William H. Danforth leading employees in song.

The Monday Morning Message

William H. Danforth, Ralston Purina's founder, had a way of keeping in touch with employees at his growing company. Called the Monday Morning Message, starting in 1921, Danforth would leave special messages on his employees' desks every Monday morning. After he passed away in 1955, his son Donald Danforth—by then the president of the company—carried on the tradition.

The messages were extremely motivational and thought-provoking for Ralston Purina employees. Long before Stephen Covey and Tony Robbins were professional career coaches, Danforth was giving out advice such as the following: "It's not easy to apologize, to begin over, to admit error, to be unselfish, to take advice, to be charitable, to be considerate, to endure success, to keep on trying, to avoid mistakes, to forgive and forget, to keep out of the rut, to make the most of a little, to maintain a high standard, to recognize the silver lining, to shoulder a deserved blame. But it always pays."

The Danforth family values were in many ways the Purina values, said W. Patrick "Pat" McGinnis, former president and CEO of Ralston Purina, who now serves as nonexecutive chairman of Nestlé Purina PetCare. "If you understand the Danforth family, they are the epitome of Midwestern values, just really good people who have honest values and believe in family and charity. We've always modeled ourselves based on the family," said McGinnis, who started working at Ralston Purina in 1972.

TURNING THE CORNER WHERE YOU ARE

The Four Talls

W
HEN WILLIAM H. DANFORTH WROTE HIS MOTIVATIONAL book in 1931, he named it *I Dare You!* The dare wasn't a threat but was, in fact, an inspiration. "Basically it was, 'I dare you to be great,'" McGinnis said. The book introduced Danforth's management philosophy, "The Four Talls." Purina employees continue to demonstrate those beliefs in their work today. Purina declares these beliefs as follows:

Stand Tall: Demonstrate integrity, pride, and dignity in your work.

Smile Tall: Show your passion about providing the highest-quality products, services, and solutions.

Think Tall: Demonstrate your expertise in the field, sharing new ideas and information.

Live Tall: Face challenges head-on to always be number one with customers.

A Fifth Tall debuted in 2009: Create Tall, to demonstrate Nestlé Purina's commitment to innovation. "We have a unique and great culture, one of high performance. And within that, there are two key aspects: integrity and continuous improvement," said Joe Sivewright, CEO of Nestlé Purina PetCare. "It goes back to Mr. Danforth's Four Talls, which we live every day. No matter what role an associate has, we all share the same passion for pets and are devoted to doing the best for them and the company. I believe our culture is a competitive advantage."

Top left: Flowers and a handshake marked Donald Danforth's promotion to president of Ralston Purina in 1932 (shown here with his father, company founder William H. Danforth).

Top right: William H. Danforth was one of the founders of the American Youth Foundation and Camp Miniwanca.

Above: William H. Danforth with his plaque about "The Four Talls."

Forging Ahead

Purina had a strong foothold in the pet food industry by the 1980s, but the company continued to evolve, always looking for the next innovation that would allow pets to thrive. That step would come with the debut of Purina's super-premium lines of food, including Pro Plan® and *Purina* ONE® in 1987.

By the 1990s, Ralston Purina no longer offered its pet foods strictly on store shelves. It was during that period that the company developed a line of exclusive pet diets sold solely through veterinarians. The products, CNM (Clinical Nutrition Management) Veterinary Diets, were followed by *Purina* Special Care—which was the first product to be granted FDA/College of Veterinary Medicine review due to its claims of reducing lower urinary tract infections in cats. Before the decade closed out, Purina launched its hypoallergenic canine diets for dogs that suffered from severe protein allergies.

"We always had a mantra that every year we wanted 20 percent of our sales to come from either improved products or totally innovative products," Pat McGinnis said. "That doesn't happen by accident. You've got to have an impressive pipeline of new ideas you're endeavoring to bring to fruition—the best formulations for the animal's health, longevity, and quality of life."

Purina's approach to innovation always has the end user at 'top of mind' said Joe Sivewright, who joined Ralston Purina in 1985. "We've always had a simple and narrowly focused approach: If it does not truly benefit the pet, the owner, or the retailer, why do it? Fortunately, that leads us into some pretty attractive areas. That's what consumers really appreciate. That gives us the ability to deploy our resources against other things in terms of working with pet owners and ensuring a positive pet-owning experience and healthy pet category."

With all of the technological advances that Ralston Purina spearheaded between its founding in 1894 and the year 2000, it's not surprising that the company attracted the attention of another powerhouse with roots in the nutrition field. By the time the country entered the new millennium, Purina was about to join forces with Nestlé and enter into a marriage that would create the premier pet nutrition company in the world.

PHOTO COURTESY OF © WHITNEY CURTIS.

Opposite: Purina encourages regular veterinary care, along with good nutrition for better pet health.

Top: Some pets wear their loyalty to Purina on their heads.

Above: Purina has a wide variety of petcare products for pet owners to choose from.

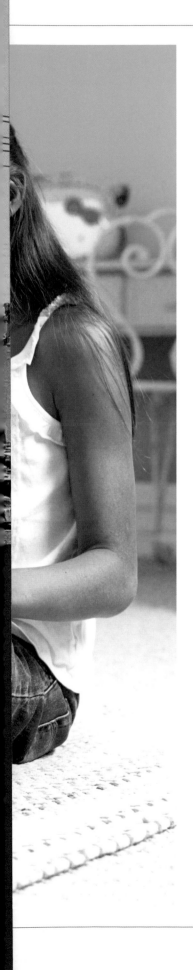

TWO POWERHOUSES UNITE

Atter more than a century in business, Ralston Purina knew the pet care industry like no other American company. By 2001, however, Purina's executives had received an intriguing query from another one of the world's most iconic brands—Nestlé®. W. Patrick "Pat" McGinnis, who was president and CEO of Ralston Purina at the time, explained how the deal came about. "Nestlé SA CEO Peter Brabeck said, 'Here's my concept: We'd like to buy you, and we're going to move our pet care unit to St. Louis, and you guys are going to run it,'" recalled McGinnis. "It wasn't something we had to argue about or negotiate or anything like that. They were terrific. I have often told people, 'If you had to be acquired, Nestlé was probably the best acquiring entity we could have hoped for.'"

The acquisition was finalized on December 12, 2001, creating Nestlé Purina® PetCare Company.

Opposite: With the proper care—like the proper nutrition from Purina—cats can live longer, happier lives.

Right: The Parque Purina in Mexico City offers a range of attractions specially designed for dogs.

Above: Purina's Beneful has a variety of product lines, including ready-to-eat dog foods and dog snacks.

Below right: Robert Hunsicker started ALPO in Pennsylvania, with a rented basement and a $200 investment, leading to such products as seen here.

Opposite top: Friskies makes its Party Mix specifically for cats.

Opposite bottom: Among the Purina brands pictured, Pro Plan is distinctive. As of 2015, the nine most recent Westminster Kennel Club Dog Show Best in Show champions were "fueled by Purina Pro Plan," and 96 of the top 100 US show dogs ate Pro Plan.

Making Room for New Products

The Nestlé/Purina merger was a significant milestone in both companies' histories. Purina forged ahead with new products, launching its Beneful® line of dog foods and treats in 2001. In addition, the merger brought iconic brands like Friskies® and ALPO® under the Purina banner, strengthening the core business.

Since the acquisition, Vella said, innovation has continued and grown. "Our consumer insights have led to highly innovative, successful products such as Purina Cat Chow® Indoor Formula and *Fancy Feast*® Elegant Medleys. Those two products alone, within 18 months, each achieved well in excess of $100 million in sales."

The newly formed company also benefited from a more robust communication strategy with the public about product benefits and advantages, the proprietary science behind those products, contributions to pet welfare and society in general, and other important topics.

"In the past, Purina didn't talk much about current performance, future business plans, or the many things we did on a daily basis to make great products and contribute to the lives of pets and the people who love them," Sivewright recalled. "But that served us well, and between that and Mr. Danforth's humble approach, we hoped that our actions would speak louder than anything else that we could do. Perhaps we didn't take credit for some of the things we should have. But now those things are very important to consumers, and we want to give them the confidence that we are doing what's right."

That transparency is valued by consumers who want the very best for their pets and who embrace the iconic Purina name every time they want to be sure they're giving their four-legged family members a new product.

> "Our consumer insights have led to highly innovative, successful products such as Purina Cat Chow Indoor Formula and Fancy Feast Elegant Medleys."
>
> — JOHN VELLA
> Senior Vice President,
> Head of Global Strategic Business
> Unit and Research & Development

1922

Abraham and Mahala Stouffer open a small dairy stand in Cleveland, beginning the family legacy of providing convenient food that tastes like homemade to consumers. By 1946, they have 15 Stouffer's restaurants in the Cleveland area.

1962

Vernon Stouffer begins supplying his restaurant's meals to grocery stores.

1973

Stouffer's joins the Nestlé SA family. Stouffer's launches its popular frozen French bread pizza in 1974.

1981

Lean Cuisine, supported by Nestlé resources in nutrition and food science, is launched and becomes a runaway success. The popularity of Lean Cuisine encourages the company to build its second "big kitchen" in Gaffney, SC.

Nestlé

1983

Brothers David and Paul Merage, owners of Chef America, introduce Hot Pockets, a hand-held pizza/sandwich combo that caters to Americans' on-the-go lifestyle. Nestlé will go on to acquire Hot Pockets in 2002.

2010

Nestle expands its frozen food offerings, adding pizza brands DiGiorno, Tombstone, Jack's, and California Pizza Kitchen, in a $3.7 billion deal with Kraft Foods.

2015

Nestlé opens a new $50 million global Research & Development Center in Solon, Ohio. The center will focus on frozen product innovation and recipe improvement to meet consumer desires and Nestlé Nutrition Foundation criteria.

2016

Tribe Mediterranean Hummus is integrated into the Nestlé USA family of products.

Stouffer's experimented with lower-calorie foods in the 1960s, but it was 1981 before it debuted Lean Cuisine (above).

In 1974, a year after joining the Nestlé family, Stouffer's launched its popular frozen French bread pizza (above center).

Stouffer's side dishes were popular, but none could eclipse macaroni and cheese (above right), which owned about 60 percent of the frozen market for that item.

Stouffer's touted the reduction in kitchen time to busy women in this 1967 ad (far right). "You now spend a daily average of just 90 minutes in the kitchen compared to the four or five hours your mother spent," the ad read.

A Gathering of Icons

Through the years, the Nestlé frozen foods family has benefited from iconic brands. Many of them were family-run, local favorites that grew over decades due to superior product quality. Taken as a whole, the brands complete much of a family's meal, from snacks to desserts.

In 1973, Stouffer's joined the Nestlé SA family. As a Nestlé family member, Stouffer's expanded quickly. In 1974, the company launched its popular frozen French bread pizza. In 1981, Lean Cuisine® went national with the tagline "You'll love the way it looks on you." The line debuted with 10 products—a culmination of testing that had begun 14 years prior.

Stouffer's: Nothing Comes Closer to Home

ABRAHAM STOUFFER AND WIFE MAHALA OPENED A SMALL DAIRY stand in Cleveland in 1922, offering a midday glass of buttermilk and free crackers. They quickly expanded the menu to include sandwiches. Mahala added her apple pie to the offerings and the restaurant eventually added dinner service. By 1946 there were 15 Stouffer's restaurants.

Changing demographics led to a Stouffer's innovation: frozen meals customers bought at restaurants and cooked later at home. "They started with macaroni and cheese," said Jim Biggar, former director of sales, general manager, and vice president of operations with Stouffer's Hotels.

In 1962, the company began supplying its frozen meals to grocery stores while it continued to expand into hotels and top-line restaurants. The convenience of frozen meals propelled Stouffer's into the 21st century.

> "Vernon Stouffer would go into the White House, go into the White House kitchen, and stock the freezer with Stouffer foods for President Eisenhower and Mamie."
>
> —BILL BIGGAR
> **Vernon Stouffer's grandson and longtime Stouffer's employee**

Above: Formerly the home of the Buitoni family, Casa Buitoni (top) is now a renowned product development center with a working test kitchen (above), demonstration workshop, and communications center in Sansepolcro, Italy.

Above right: Today Buitoni makes it possible for American families to eat quality Italian food at home.

Inset: Buitoni makes pasta and sauce products like this Sweet Bell Pepper & Roasted Chicken Ravioli.

Buitoni®: All the Freshness of Little Italy

As one would want from a pasta empire, the Buitoni story is filled with both passion and heart. Guilia and Giovanbattista Buitoni sold Guilia's pearls and mortgaged two acres of farmland to fund their pasta business in Italy in 1827. The modest factory quickly became a family business, with their children opening additional factories between Florence and Rome. Buitoni continued to expand in Italy, starting the Perugina brand and establishing the Perugina® Chocolate Factory in 1907.

But it wasn't until World War II, when Giovani and Letizia Buitoni were stranded in the United States by the war in Europe, that Americans first got a taste of their pasta. The Buitonis launched an American arm of the business while they rode out the war stateside. Carrying on the family tradition, Letizia Buitoni pawned her jewelry to fund the US venture, which made its debut at the 1939 World's Fair in New York.

The Buitoni and Perugina brands merged in 1969 under the name Industrie Buitoni Perugina (IBP), with a focus on a more formal United States expansion. By 1980, Americans' love of pasta had intensified and Nestlé purchased Buitoni in 1988 for $1.27 billion, introducing the Buitoni® brand of authentic Italian cooking to Americans shortly thereafter.

Hot Pockets® Joins a Growing Family

WHILE NOT QUITE AS LONG AND STORIED A HISTORY AS Nestlé's other frozen foods, *Hot Pockets* was equally revolutionary. Chef America, founded by David and Paul Merage, created the frozen sandwich/pizza combination in 1977. The product quickly became popular, especially once it was offered in retail stores. *Hot Pockets* was the only hot sandwich that came with a microwave-crisping sleeve to give their crusts a crunchy texture. In 1987, the company launched Lean Pockets® to meet consumers' interest in healthier foods. When Nestlé purchased the company in 2002, it had $750 million in annual sales.

"The Hot Pockets and Lean Pockets brands have anticipated culinary trends and built an interactive relationship with loyal consumers through innovative, quality products for more than 30 years."

—JOHN CARMICHAEL
President,
Pizza & Snacking Division

Nestlé acquired Hot Pockets (top) in 2002. In 1987, the company added Lean Pockets (left) to the product line.

1921

William Dreyer opens a creamery in Visalia, California, winning the 1921 Pacific Slope Dairy Show. Later, Dreyer and Joseph Edy, a candy parlor owner, create "Grand" Ice cream. Dreyer makes the ice cream that Edy sells in his candy parlors.

1928

I. C. Parker, advertising manager for the Pangburn Candy and Ice Cream Company, invents a new ice cream novelty. The chocolate- and nut-dipped ice cream cone is frozen, and then wrapped before sale. His wife, Jewel, is said to have noted the cone's resemblance to a fried chicken leg, giving rise to the new treat's name: Drumstick.

1929

Eighteen-year-old Reuben Mattus, along with his mother and sister, launches a line of frozen confections called Senator Food Products, the precursor to Häagen-Dazs. Mattus sells his wares from a horse-drawn cart.

1977

William "Rick" Cronk and Gary Rogers purchase Dreyer's and expand the company beyond Northern California. Eventually Dreyer's is sold throughout the country.

1983

Jan Booth invents Dreyer's Grand Light ice cream. Despite having a much lower fat content, the ice cream has the same texture and quality as Dreyer's regular ice cream. It becomes Dreyer's biggest new product.

1994

Skinny Cow ice cream is created by two New York beer distributors. Later the brand expands to include other kinds of low-calorie snacks.

1999

Nestlé begins a joint venture with Häagen-Dazs, and the brand was officially licensed to Nestlé in 2001.

2002

Nestlé acquires Dreyer's, making it the biggest ice cream maker in the United States.

WE ALL SCREAM FOR ICE CREAM

EVERY FAMILY MEAL NEEDS A DESSERT, AND NESTLÉ CERTAINLY HAS plenty to offer, including ice cream. Dreyer's®/Edy's® and Häagen-Dazs® are the centerpieces of Nestlé in the US ice cream offerings. The company also offers Nestlé®-brand novelties like Drumstick® and Outshine®.

In 1999, Dreyer's formed a joint venture with Nestlé; the company already had been distributing Nestlé novelties through its vast distribution network. In 2002, Nestlé purchased the remainder of the company.

Häagen-Dazs was a super-premium category ice cream brand developed by Reuben Mattus and his wife Rose in their ice cream shop in Brooklyn, New York. "They invented the name, Häagen-Dazs," Rick Cronk explained, "which has no actual meaning, and sounds Scandinavian. It was brilliant!" Häagen-Dazs was sold to Pillsbury in 1983. In 1999, Pillsbury aligned with Nestlé for distribution. Nestlé took full ownership in 2002 of a product mix that expanded to include frozen yogurt, gelato, and bars.

Nestlé ownership has enabled each of these brands to expand and adapt to meet a changing flavor palate. Dreyer's/Edy's added a slow-churned ice cream, which had less fat but the same rich taste. Häagen-Dazs also added an extra-rich light ice cream. In 2004, Nestlé purchased another lighter product, Skinny Cow®, created by two New York beer distributors in the early 1990s.

Right: Cookies 'n Cream Truffle Bar is just one of the many sumptuous Skinny Cow flavors available.

Above: William Dreyer (top) and Joseph Edy (above) changed the way Americans eat ice cream.

Above right: Dreyer's has been a part of family and social gatherings for generations.

Below: William Dreyer invented Rocky Road ice cream in 1929 to "calm his nerves" after the stock market crash that launched the Great Depression.

Dreyer's: Share a Scoop, Share a Smile

Dreyer's was launched somewhere in the Atlantic Ocean as young galley boy William Dreyer was given the task of making a frozen dessert to cap the final night of the voyage on the SS *Kaiser Wilhelm*. His fruit-based "water ice" proved popular with the guests, and the 18-year-old decided he would pursue ice cream once in America.

That was 1906. By 1910, Dreyer was in California, where he honed his craft working for others.

In 1921, Dreyer opened his own creamery in Visalia, California, winning the 1921 Pacific Slope Dairy Show. When Dreyer met Joseph Edy, a candy parlor owner, they created "Grand" ice cream.

Dreyer and Edy opened a small factory in Oakland in 1928. Dreyer made the ice cream that Edy sold in his candy parlors. Their combined knowledge of candy and ice cream led to the development of new flavors, like Rocky Road, which Dreyer created to "calm his nerves" after the stock market crash that launched the Great Depression. The name came from what lay ahead for America: a rocky road. Because only large marshmallows were manufactured at the time, William Dreyer used his wife's sewing scissors to cut marshmallows into bite-sized pieces to make the first batch of Rocky Road.

That road may not have been smooth, but for Dreyer, it proved successful. The Great Depression caused business owners to seek out new revenue streams. Dreyer wanted to bring ice cream out of specialty stores and into the mass market. After Dreyer's son William Jr. returned from World War II, father and son focused on ice cream manufacturing.

The tiny Piedmont Grocery located in Piedmont, California saw an opportunity for its customers, and asked Bill Dreyer if he might consider packaging his ice cream in quart or half-gallon containers for sale in the grocery store. Bill Dreyer thought that was a splendid idea, but Edy thought it might hurt trade within their own stores. Edy was consumed with expanding his candy operation, and the two dissolved the partnership and Grand Ice Cream became Dreyer's Grand Ice Cream®.

After William Dreyer retired in 1953, William Jr. expanded into diners. A decade later, he sold the company to three of its officers, who focused on maintaining the quality while making it available to the masses. Then in 1977, William "Rick" Cronk and Gary Rogers purchased the company and took Dreyer's to new heights, expanding beyond Northern California and throughout the country.

"*Dreyer's Grand Ice Cream* was packaged in round white containers," Cronk recalled, "while everything else was in bricks and squares." Another novel feature was that the cartons had a "see-though" top which made the brand very appealing to consumers. Dreyer's was rebranded Edy's® in Midwest and Eastern markets.

One of the most important business decisions that Cronk and Rogers made was to maintain direct store delivery (DSD) of Dreyer's products. "We began to appreciate the luck or genius of Bill Dreyer in terms of independent distribution," Cronk remembered. DSD meant that every Dreyer's product was delivered directly to the grocery store in one of Dreyer's own freezer trucks, and would never endure the high temperatures of the loading dock coming from a supermarket's own warehouses. It was a commitment to quality which is maintained to this day. "We didn't sell one half-gallon of ice cream in the entire 30 years I was there that didn't come off our own trucks," Rogers declared.

In about 1983, Jan Booth joined the company, becoming the first vice president of marketing, and soon "invented Dreyer's Grand Light®," Cronk explained, "which was a much lower fat ice cream but of the same texture and quality as our regular ice cream. *Grand Light* was a huge success. It was singularly the biggest new product that we ever created."

This page: Nestlé ice cream has something to please every palate with kitchen-friendly ingredients, from Dreyer's multiple offerings (above) to Outshine Fruit Bars (below).

Häagen-Dazs was created in 1960 by Reuben and Rose Mattus in their Bronx apartment. Its Danish-sounding name (and the outline of Denmark on the lid) was used to create an aura of European luxury.

Häagen-Dazs: The Source for Pure Pleasure

WHILE DREYER'S WAS GROWING ON THE WEST COAST, A young Italian ice seller was getting started in the East. Reuben Mattus started selling lemon ices in Brooklyn at the age of 10. By 1929, 18-year-old Reuben, along with his mother and sister, launched a line of frozen confections called Senator Food Products, delivered from a horse-drawn cart.

When Reuben, who by then had been joined by wife Rose, noticed that customers preferred the company's ices better than their ice creams, he hit the books, studying how to improve his ice cream making.

Clearly, something worked. By the 1950s, his experimentation had led to a higher butterfat content, making the ice cream richer. Reuben and Rose showed their marketing skills were as superior as their ice creams. They thought if they tapped into a European-sounding name, Americans would be more impressed. Häagen-Dazs was born.

While they intended to launch with the standard chocolate, vanilla, and strawberry flavors, Reuben felt that the strawberry was not up to his high standards. He added a coffee flavor to the line instead. He traveled the world, sourcing the best ingredients, like dark chocolate from Belgium and vanilla from Madagascar.

By 1973, Häagen-Dazs had nationwide distribution, and within a few years had launched a chain of scoop shops.

Dreyer's was the first to introduce a lower fat ice cream in the United States. Another landmark success was the introduction of "slow churned" ice cream in the late 1990s. "We got all kinds of patents on it," Gary Rogers recalled, "and today it accounts for more than half of Dreyer's total sales. It was a huge success."

In 2002, Nestlé acquired Dreyer's, making it the largest ice cream maker in the United States. "I know that Americans eat more ice cream than any country in the world," Dick Cronk said, "and it's something like 24 gallons a year!"

Nestlé Novelties

Nestlé Drumstick® grew from the St. Louis World's Fair in 1904, which was marked by the introduction of the ice cream cone. In 1928, I. C. Parker, advertising manager for the Pangburn Candy and Ice Cream Company in Fort Worth, Texas, took that World's Fair innovation to the grocery stores. Workers hand-filled cones and placed them in a "hardening room" to freeze solid. They were then dipped in chocolate, nuts, and wrapped. In the 1930s, the *Drumstick* made its way into the grocery store.

Legend has it that *Drumsticks* got their name when Parker's wife Jewel remarked that the new ice cream treat looked like a fried chicken leg. Thus, the name "*Drumstick*."

Since its creation, *Drumsticks* are even tastier. The cone now has a chocolate lining and a dollop of chocolate at the bottom. The treats come in three different sizes and are available with or without nuts. In 1991, Drumstick added Push-Up® treats to its line when it joined Nestlé.

Nestlé has had its own success with novelties, many of which feature other Nestlé products. Fans of Nestlé confections can indulge in familiar brands such as Nestlé Crunch®, Baby Ruth®, and Butterfinger® ice cream bars. And Nestlé Toll House® Chocolate Chip Cookie Sandwich became an instant best seller when it was first introduced.

For Nestlé ice cream, the future looks delicious.

Above: Nestlé Drumstick, The Original Sundae Cone, has a variety of flavor and size combinations.

Below: Nestlé's rich, creamy ice cream comes in a variety of forms and flavors.

1951

Dr. Lewis J. Minor, a food scientist, founds the L. J. Minor Corporation in Cleveland with $6,000 and a borrowed mixer. His company is the first manufacturer to create refrigerated, meat-first, food-based stock.

1952

Dr. Minor hires chefs to sell his product, enforcing the company's idea that the product was created by chefs, for chefs. Minor sees his company as "partners with the professional chefs and cooks of America."

1977

Thanks in part to the efforts of L. J. Minor Corp., the US Department of Labor and the American Culinary Federation announce that the role of executive chef is moving from the "services" category to the "professional, technical, and managerial occupations" category in the *Dictionary of Official Titles*.

1984

L. J. Minor Corp. is the first US manufacturer to win Grand Gold at the Culinary Olympics in Germany. The top award comes after Minor's eight-member team earns seven gold medals and one silver in the restaurant and individual plate categories.

1985

L. J. Minor Corp. joins Nestlé, bringing with it a portfolio of hundreds of products that make a chef's day easier.

2008

Nestlé Professional takes a huge step forward, launching the Customer Innovation Campus, a 67,000-square-foot facility with a flexible kitchen design. This enables visiting food professionals to mirror their own operations, allowing products to be developed seamlessly and then transferred back to their restaurant kitchen.

2009

Nestlé acquires restaurant beverage firm Vitality Foods. Vitality's juices, teas, coffees, and smoothies join other popular restaurant beverage items such as Nescafé and Coffee-mate.

2015

JULY
Nestlé proudly opens a new Research and Development Center in Solon, Ohio.

NESTLÉ
CHEF 2 CHEF

THE NESTLÉ PROFESSIONAL STORY IS DEEPLY ENTWINED WITH THAT OF Nestlé in the US. Nestlé offers consumers so many beloved products on grocery shelves, it was only natural that the company would eventually offer the same delicious, high-quality, consistent flavors to chefs and restaurant operators. When a cafeteria serves Libby's® pumpkin pie or a national restaurant chain offers a Butterfinger® brownie sundae on the menu, you can see the benefit of Nestlé Professional.

Over the years, Nestlé Professional has partnered with operators to reflect and delight the American palate. Nestlé Professional is focused on working hand-in-hand with chefs and operators to deliver the best flavor in every dish. It is the culmination of a partnership with professional chefs that dates back throughout Nestlé history.

Opposite: The Nestlé Professional Customer Innovation Campus in Solon, Ohio, features a 67,000-square-foot facility with a customizable commercial kitchen.

Right: Minor's provides many products to professional kitchens, such as these stocks.

Right: L. J. Minor Corp. representatives Jean Caubet and Eric Swanson participated in a 1950s tradeshow display.

Below: Mr. and Mrs. L. J. Minor pose with their son Michael L. Minor, an accomplished professional chef.

Minor's: Flavor Means Business

Some of the best-known Nestlé brands got their start—or at least significant exposure—in the restaurant industry. The Stouffer Corporation, for instance, began as a creamery that soon expanded to a dairy stand that sold buttermilk and crackers. Later, Stouffer's added sandwiches to the menu. That grew into full restaurants and hotels in the 1960s.

Dr. Lewis J. Minor took another approach, developing products for out-of-home use. Minor, a food scientist, founded the L. J. Minor Company in Cleveland, Ohio, with $6,000 and a borrowed mixer. He was the first manufacturer to create refrigerated meat-first, food-based stock. A year later, in 1952, he hired chefs to sell his product, enforcing the company's idea that the product was created by chefs, for chefs. He saw his company as "partners with the professional chefs and cooks of America."

Never leaving its chef roots far behind, in 1984, L. J. Minor Corp. was the first US manufacturer to win Grand Gold [above left] at the Culinary Olympics in Germany. The top award came after Minor's eight-member team earned seven gold medals and one silver in the restaurant and individual plate categories.

Minor's joined Nestlé in 1985, bringing with it a portfolio of hundreds of products that would make a chef's day easier.

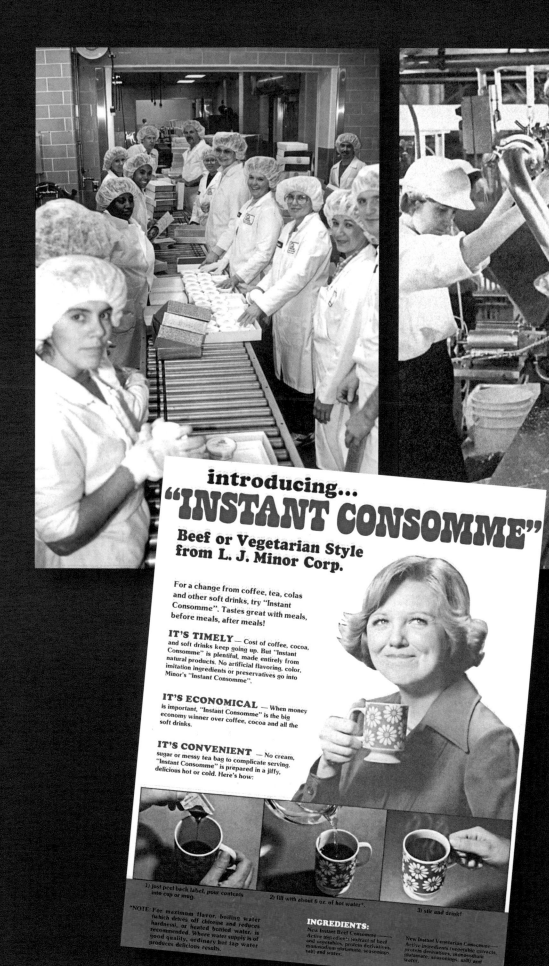

introducing...

"INSTANT CONSOMME"

**Beef or Vegetarian Style
from L. J. Minor Corp.**

For a change from coffee, tea, colas
and other soft drinks, try "Instant
Consomme". Tastes great with meals,
before meals, after meals!

IT'S TIMELY — Cost of coffee, cocoa,
and soft drinks keep going up. But "Instant
Consomme" is plentiful, made entirely from
natural products. No artificial flavoring, color,
imitation ingredients or preservatives go into
Minor's "Instant Consomme".

IT'S ECONOMICAL — When money
is important, "Instant Consomme" is the big
economy winner over coffee, cocoa and all the
soft drinks.

IT'S CONVENIENT — No cream,
sugar or messy tea bag to complicate serving.
"Instant Consomme" is prepared in a jiffy,
delicious hot or cold. Here's how:

1) Just peel back label, pour contents
into cup or mug.

2) fill with about 6 oz. of hot water*.

3) stir and drink!

*NOTE: For maximum flavor, boiling water
(which drives off chlorine and reduces
hardness), or heated bottled water, is
recommended. Where water supply is of
good quality, ordinary hot tap water
produces delicious results.

INGREDIENTS:
New Instant Beef Consomme —
Active ingredients (extract of beef
and vegetables, protein derivatives,
monosodium glutamate, seasonings,
salt) and water.

New Instant Vegetarian Consomme —
Active ingredients (vegetable extracts,
protein derivatives, monosodium
glutamate, seasonings, salt) and
water.

Above left: Workers put
products into
packaging material.

Above right: Salinas, California
plant workers carefully
monitor mixtures during
the processing stage.

Left: An early ad for consomme
touted it as an alternative to
coffee, tea, or cola.

Nestlé Professional chefs work with food product experts to bring a multitude of flavors to United States consumers.

Nestlé Professional Comes Together

Nestlé continued to expand its offerings to the out-of-home market. While Minor's provided product to support a chef's creation—such as bases and stocks—Chef-mate® offered a variety of sauces and finished products that could be customized before serving while offering consistent, delicious flavors. In 2009, the restaurant beverage firm Vitality Foods joined Nestlé. Nestlé then had Vitality's juices, teas, coffees, and smoothies in addition to other popular restaurant beverage items such as Nescafé® and Coffee-mate®.

It Started With a Dairy Stand

A SMALL DAIRY STAND OFFERING BUTTERMILK AND CRACKERS IN 1922 grew into a business empire. Abraham and Mahala Stouffer first offered sandwiches for lunch. Then they offered dinner. That led to the restaurant business and, later, the hotel industry. The family's food was so good, people asked for frozen portions to take home for later. By the mid-1950s, the Stouffers were in the frozen-food business with a dedicated processing plant. Today, Stouffer's is part of Nestlé in the US and produces more than 150 kinds of premium-quality frozen prepared foods.

Above: The Stouffer family started their restaurant chain in the 1930s. This image shows the interior of a restaurant from the late 1960s or early 1970s.

Right: Stouffer's frozen food packaging focused on entrees rather than entire meals.

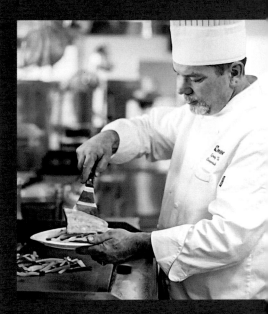

By the turn of the twenty-first century, it made sense to bring these food service divisions together. Product development teams from Stouffer's, L. J. Minor, and Nestlé merged into one unit. In 2008, Nestlé Professional took a huge step forward, launching the Customer Innovation Campus, a 67,000-square-foot facility with a flexible kitchen design. Visiting food professionals could mirror their own operations, demonstrating products to be developed seamlessly and then transferred back to their restaurant kitchen.

"Collaboration begins by connecting to operators. We offer solutions to the pain-points they experience in their daily operations. Our Chef 2 Chef brigade can help with innovation, offering healthier recipes, sharing trends in flavors, menu items, or techniques. We are partners with our customers—we want to understand how we can work with them," said Perry Miele, president, regional business head for Nestlé Professional North America for food.

These activities don't always happen on campus. "We have tremendous resources available to us. We can really partner with key flavor suppliers all over the globe. We take individuals on treks to places to see where things are sourced and what's out there," said Carol Stropki, product development manager. "We're going so deep in understanding how spices are grown, how they're harvested, and the sustainability side of things. There's always a new angle on spices or flavors that you didn't think was important before."

Partnering with Nestlé Professional means chefs have an opportunity to explore new flavors while Nestlé handles the supply chain vetting to ensure products are safe. Nestlé and the chefs then work together to influence and drive new flavor trends.

> "Nestlé Professional is special because we don't just focus on one product or one aspect of the business. We focus on the needs of our customer—every day. We're in food service, we help the operator delight consumers, because their success is our success."
>
> —PERRY MIELE
> President, Nestlé Professional
> North America–Food

Left and above: Nestlé Professional offers new flavors from all over the world for chefs to incorporate in their professional kitchens.

Top: Corporate executive chefs serve a tasting lunch at the Nestlé Professional Customer Innovation Campus in Solon, Ohio.

Inset: The 200-pound plaque memorializing Dr. L. J. Minor, Chef Louis Szathmary, and General John McLaughlin for their efforts in changing the status of chefs to professionals.

A Professional Profession

I N TERMS OF GOVERNMENT CATEGORIES, CHEFS WERE CATEGORIZED THE same as domestics. Dr. L. J. Minor worked very hard to make the chef title a professional job classification. During a 1974 speech at the American Culinary Federation Convention, Chef Louis I. Szathmary called on Americans to raise the profile of the profession. Lieutenant General John McLaughlin, then president of L. J. Minor Corp., accepted the challenge. Dr. Minor made significant contributions from the company funds to support the effort. It was not an unusual move for the company, which had long supported such professional endeavors. Minor Corp. had supported the American Culinary Federation since 1970, and in 1972 established loan funds for Johnson and Wales University, which featured a significant culinary arts program.

In 1977, the US Department of Labor and the American Culinary Federation announced that the role of executive chef would move from the "services" category to the "professional, technical, and managerial occupations" category in the *Dictionary of Official Titles.*

In 1983, the Culinary Institute of America dedicated a classroom to Dr. Minor. Some 30 years later, the American Culinary Federation named its highest honor after Dr. Minor. Beginning in 2013, the Dr. L. J. Minor Chef Professionalism Award recognized a chef who exemplified the highest standard of professionalism through continuing education and community involvement.

Different Flavors Drive Innovation

"We work directly with restauranteurs to develop new products," Miele said. "People try new things when they eat out, first. They try a new flavor and say, 'Wow, that's fantastic.' All trends get started in food service; that is where the innovation happens. Some chef looks at a flavor and introduces a new dish. We're not experimenting, we're delivering foods from different parts of the world and bringing them together to inspire and delight consumers with new flavors."

That, in turn, helps create demand. "That's what we can tap into, all our food service network and research and development networks around the world to bring that together," Miele said. "That's what's special here in the United States with the Nestlé Professional Customer Innovation Campus (NPCIC)."

Creations that happen at the NPCIC are truly the result of a partnership between operators and the talented Nestlé Professional team. "We're accessing our global network of research and development personnel to find regional and global trends," Stropki said. "In the past five years, especially, we have been focused on more regional flavors and dishes. We're sourcing locally and adding global cuisine, unique flavors, and launching new trends for the out-of-home diner. Trends and new cuisines almost always start in restaurants—we have access to global resources that benefit our customers. That's what makes Nestlé special."

Nestlé Professional strives to be the trusted partner of choice by providing category expertise and innovative, profitable food and beverage solutions that help our customers win.

Below left and above: The operations kitchen at Nestlé Professional allows a chef to duplicate their own kitchen setup to test new recipes and techniques.

Below: Nestlé chefs prepare food on the state-of-the-art Customer Innovation Campus.

Nestlé

1947

Cetaphil Cleansing Lotion is invented by a pharmacist and launched by Texas Pharmacal in San Antonio, Texas.

1961

Owen Dermatology opens in Dallas, Texas.

1981

Nestlé & L'Oréal form a joint venture solely dedicated to dermatology: Galderma.

1998

Inauguration of a new research and development (R&D) facility in Princeton, New Jersey. In 2015, the R&D center relocates to Nestlé Skin Health US headquarters in Fort Worth, Texas, and New York City.

2008

Acquisition of CollaGenex Pharmaceuticals and its product Oracea Capsules.

2011

Galderma acquires Q-Med, a Swedish company specializing in aesthetic and corrective solutions.

2013

Galderma acquires the Swiss company Spirig Pharma AG, manufacturer of Daylong sunscreen products and Excipial skincare line.

2014

Nestlé Skin Health is created as part of a commitment by Nestlé to expand the boundaries of Nutrition, Health and Wellness. The company grows out of Galderma, the dermatology joint venture founded with L'Oréal in 1981.

MEETING LIFELONG SKIN HEALTH NEEDS

THE SKIN IS THE LARGEST ORGAN IN THE HUMAN BODY. AS THE external indicator of our internal wellness, healthy skin can have a positive impact on our well-being, which is why we must focus not only on treating and restoring it, but also on maintaining it and enhancing its qualities.

Nestlé Skin Health was created in 2014 as part of a commitment by Nestlé to expand the boundaries of Nutrition, Health and Wellness. The company grew out of Galderma, the dermatology joint venture founded with L'Oréal in 1981.

Nestlé Skin Health's mission is to enhance the quality of life by delivering science-based solutions for the health of skin, hair, and nails. As a leader, Nestlé Skin Health conducts groundbreaking research to provide both the health care community and the consumer with an ongoing progression of innovative technologies and products to protect, serve, and enhance skin health.

Nestlé Skin Health

Opposite: Nestlé Skin Health is supported by five research and development centers located around the world: France, Japan, Sweden, Switzerland, and the United States.

The company partners with health care professionals around the world to meet the skin health needs of people throughout their lifetime. Galderma is a leader in research and development of scientifically defined and medically proven solutions for skin, hair, and nails.

Image supplied by Nestlé

Nestlé Skin Health may be a relatively new venture, but its roots run deep. Owen Dermatology traces its origins back to 1961 in Dallas. When Nestlé and L'Oréal formed a joint venture in 1981, the Galderma product line was not far behind, focused on skin diseases such as acne, rosacea, psoriasis, pigmentary disorders, fungal nail infections, and skin cancers.

In 1995, Galderma launched Differin® Gel on the global market. It is the first product to emerge from Galderma's own research efforts. Products quickly followed, and North America became Galderma's largest market.

Over the next decade, Galderma continued to acquire new products, bring global products to the US market, and create innovative solutions.

Nestlé Skin Health is a true leader in the field of research and development (R&D) in dermatology. More than 700 researchers in R&D facilities in France, Sweden, and Switzerland, and in their Clinical Development centers in Japan, Switzerland, Sweden, France, and the United States are committed to finding innovative solutions to meet people's skin health needs.

Today, Nestlé Skin Health employs approximately 6,000 people worldwide, and its science-based solutions are present in more than 100 countries across the globe.

By partnering with health care professionals and institutions around the world, Galderma strives to build and sustain a strong and long-lasting dermatology community. Thanks to a number of social responsibility and educational initiatives, Galderma is contributing to growing a responsible dermatology community, which will advance dermatological medicine and improve the lives of people suffering from dermatological diseases.

"I am proud to be part of a company consistently trusted by doctors and patients that is truly changing people's lives with its solutions for skin health."

—MILES HARRISON
President and General Manager
of Galderma North America

Strategic brands in the United States include Epiduo® Gel, Epiduo® Forte Gel, Oracea® Capsules, Clobex® Spray, Differin® Gel, Mirvaso® Gel, MetroGel® Gel, Soolantra® Cream, Vectical® Cream, Tri-Luma® Cream, Cetaphil®, Benzac® Acne Solutions, Excipial™ Skin Solutions, Qilib™, Restylane®, Restylane® Silk, Restylane® Lyft, Dysport® (abobotulinumtoxin A), and Sculptra® Aesthetic.

Cetaphil®: The Gentle Choice

ONE OF THE OLDEST AND MOST WIDELY USED BRANDS IN THE SKIN Health portfolio, *Cetaphil* was developed by a pharmacist in 1947. The product initially was only available through select pharmacists but quickly gained the attention of dermatologists, pediatricians, and other health care professionals as an effective method of treating common skin conditions.

Cetaphil became more widely available in the 1980s, selling in major retail chains across North America.

While the brand has expanded into a number of products, the *Cetaphil* Gentle Skin Cleanser still uses the original formula developed in 1947.

Cetaphil's Gentle Power is available to clean and moisturize the skin of both adults and babies. The product may be purchased as a cleanser, moisturizing cream, and skin-cleansing cloths.

"Our goal is to grow the number of people the company serves to over a billion within 10 years, by offering skin health solutions that protect, maintain, nourish, and enhance skin health and, when skin health is compromised, treat, correct, and restore the skin to its healthy state."

—HUMBERTO C. ANTUNES
CEO of Nestlé Skin Health, SA and
Chairman of the Board of Directors
of Galderma Pharma, SA

Nestlé Skin Health is establishing an international network of innovation hubs known as Nestlé Skin Health Investigation, Education, and Longevity Development (SHIELD) centers.

Nestlé Skin Health Investigation, Education, and Longevity Development: SHIELD Centers

In response to the expected rise in skin health needs in a rapidly growing and aging population, Nestlé Skin Health has started to establish a global network of innovation hubs to advance the next generation of skin health. Known as the Nestlé Skin Health Investigation, Education, and Longevity Development (SHIELD) centers, this global innovation network will be built to foster breakthroughs and collaboration in skin health through medical investigation, education, and applications related to the convergence of technologies and bio-informatics.

SHIELD is looking for boundary-breakers, thinkers, dreamers, and visionaries to inspire a global, multidisciplinary collective, where creative minds come together. Physicians, nurses, clinicians, caregivers, scientists, entrepreneurs, tech leaders, academic partners, and advocacy groups across the health care and aging innovation continuum are invited to join the SHIELD centers platform and work together to advance skin health.

The first SHIELD center, in New York, opened in Spring 2016.

Solutions for a Broad Range of Skin Health Needs

Nestlé Skin Health is a global leader focused on meeting the world's increasing skin health needs with a broad range of innovative and scientifically proven products. These products, which include solutions for skin, hair, and nails, are available from physicians or in local stores.

PRESCRIPTION SOLUTIONS

SELF-MEDICATION SOLUTIONS

AESTHETIC & CORRECTIVE SOLUTIONS

CONSUMER SOLUTIONS

"Our mindset with our aesthetic treatments is really about helping people achieve the best version of themselves; to feel empowered. It's about helping them to discover their best self as an expression of wellness."

—VIRGINIE NAIGEON
Corporate Communications Director
for Galderma in North America

1989

Nestlé forms a joint venture with Clintec (Nestlé Clinical Nutrition, Deerfield, Illinois). Clintec will be dissolved in 1996, but Nestlé will retain the Enteral Nutrition business.

2003–2007

Nestlé Clinical Nutrition headquarters moves to Glendale, California, and becomes part of Nestlé Nutrition Division. In 2007, Nestlé acquires Novartis Medical Nutrition and becomes a strong number two player in Medical Nutrition in the United States.

2010

The Nestlé HealthCare Nutrition business acquires Vitaflo and its portfolio of clinical nutritional solutions for inherited metabolic disorders.

2011

Nestlé forms Nestlé Health Science as a wholly-owned subsidiary and transfers the HealthCare Nutrition business from Nestlé Nutrition to form the foundation of the new company. Nestlé also establishes the Nestlé Institute of Health Sciences (part of the Nestlé R&D Network).

HEALTH SCIENCE

2011

Nestlé Health Science acquires Prometheus, a leading US diagnostic and therapeutic company active in GI and oncology.

2013

Nestlé Health Science acquires Pamlab, with a portfolio addressing nutritional needs related to depression, diabetic peripheral neuropathy, and cognitive impairment.

2015

Nestlé Health Science invests in Seres Health, with a pipeline of first-generation microbiome therapeutics.

2016–2017

Nestlé sets up the Product Technology Center dedicated to Nestlé Health Science in Bridgewater, New Jersey. The Center will focus on accelerating innovative nutritional solutions to improve health care.

FOR BETTER HEALTH

N ESTLÉ HAS MAINTAINED A NUTRITION, HEALTH, AND WELLNESS strategy since its inception. When the company acquired Novartis Medical Nutrition and its portfolio of health care brands in 2007, the combination made the company a nutritional powerhouse. Nestlé established Nestlé Health Science in 2011 and transferred what had been known as the Nestlé HealthCare Nutrition business to the new company to form its foundation. Today, the employees of Nestlé Health Science share a singular commitment to helping patients and consumers lead healthier lives every day.

With the 2015 announcement to establish a Nestlé Product Technology Center (NPTC) dedicated to Nestlé Health Science in Bridgewater, New Jersey during 2016–2017, the company is committed to deepening the role of nutrition in health care, an area that is rich in innovation potential, as more is learned about the roles of nutrients in addressing health needs.

Opposite: Nestlé Health Science shares a singular commitment to helping patients and consumers lead healthier lives every day.

Right: Carnation Breakfast Essentials has helped time-challenged families get delicious, nutritious meals for more than 50 years, when it was originally marketed as Carnation Instant Breakfast.

Introduced in 1965 as Carnation Instant Breakfast (above), the Carnation Breakfast Essentials family (below) includes powdered mixes and ready-to-drink bottles. Carnation Breakfast Essentials provides the nutrition of a balanced breakfast.

Good Nutrition from the Start

Many American Baby Boomers remember the Carnation Instant Breakfast Drink commercials from the 1960s and 1970s, but not quite as many people were buying the products by the time the brand became part of the Nestlé Health Science banner in 2008.

Patrick Todd, vice president of marketing for the consumer care business of Nestlé Health Science in the United States and Canada, had ambitious plans for reinvigorating the now 50-year-old brand.

Seeing potential in the fact that many dietitians and hospitals recommended the product for nutritional purposes, Nestlé Health Science chose to focus on its nutritional value. "We took a look at a lot of the old creative and marketing material, and it was really positioned around, 'Well, it's better than skipping breakfast,'" Todd said. The team's research revealed that the brand had awareness among 85 percent of Americans, but consumers could barely remember the last time they had consumed it for breakfast. The team talked to health care professionals and pediatricians, who spotlighted the fact that teenagers weren't getting the essential proteins and vitamins that they needed for a good start to the day, and they came up with the tagline, "Good nutrition from the start."

Nestlé Health Science changed the product's name to Carnation Breakfast Essentials® and made inroads with health care professionals and parents, stressing how the product helped consumers meet the need for a nutritious breakfast. After putting the new branding and messaging on television, sales began to climb.

"It's been continuous double-digit growth year-on-year, and I attribute a lot of that to just having a focused target group with sound messaging around nutrition," Todd said. Nestlé Health Science also debuted a new ready-to-drink product in bottles that outperformed the competition in that category.

PHOTO COURTESY OF STEVEN PETERS / THE IMAGE BANK COLLECTION / GETTY IMAGES.

Facing Challenges Head-On

Nestlé Health Science is acutely aware of the pressure of health care reform on health care professionals and patients today. As insurance payments shrink and premiums rise, customers want the highest-quality products at the lowest possible price more than ever, said Anna Mohl, regional business head for the Medical Nutrition business for Nestlé Health Science in North America.

"We've made investments in our products in terms of launching innovation, in terms of our factory, in terms of moving to aseptic manufacturing," Mohl said. Aseptic manufacturing allows for the sterile and safe packaging of the company's products. These investments fit into an overall plan for better health outcomes while keeping costs reasonable.

"The idea is to improve the quality of care in population health while reducing the cost of care. Hospitals and physicians are going to more evidence-based solutions where you need to have data that shows that you'll have a better outcome, both clinically as well as financially, from using a particular product."

Nestlé Health Science manufactures a variety of nutritional products that doctors, patients, and caregivers trust at an affordable price.

Stay Stong, Stay Active with BOOST

BOOST drinks are available in many varieties, including Original, Calorie Smart, Glucose Control, and High Protein. Consumers can enjoy three flavors of BOOST Original Drink: Rich Chocolate (pictured), Very Vanilla, and Creamy Strawberry.

Walk into any grocery store, and just a few aisles away from *Carnation Breakfast Essentials* you'll find packs of *BOOST*, Nestlé Health Science's biggest brand. "*BOOST* is a nutritionally complete drink serving the health and wellness needs of people aged 50 plus," said Barbara McCartney, regional business head for the consumer care business in the United States and Canada for Nestlé Health Science.

The product was originally developed as a way for people to get the nutrients they need that they are not able to get from their diet alone, which makes it a top go-to product for health care professionals,

"With the pressure on cost of care driven by health care reform, health care professionals and customers want the highest quality of products at the lowest possible price ... We've taken a really hard look at different product segments and categories within our portfolio and [asked] ... 'Which are the ones that really add value that we can differentiate ourselves?'"

—ANNA MOHL
Regional Business Head
for the Medical Nutrition business
for Nestlé Health Science
in North America

McCartney said. Today, half of the BOOST brand's volume results from a patient's interaction with a physician or a dietitian. "They trust the product because of its long-standing quality of nutrition," she said. "They trust it because it's used in hospitals, and they trust it because of Nestlé and the quality reputation that Nestlé has as a food company."

The BOOST brand, which joined Nestlé Health Science during the Novartis Medical Nutrition acquisition in 2007, is growing quickly and comprises a significant portion of Nestlé Health Science's revenues in the United States.

PHOTO COURTESY OF © BOHM-MARRAZZO STUDIOS.

Above: Nestlé Health Science creates nutritional products to help improve individuals' nutrition, or to help manage a specific disease or condition. Sensory research is an important part of innovation to assure these products also deliver a superior sensory experience.

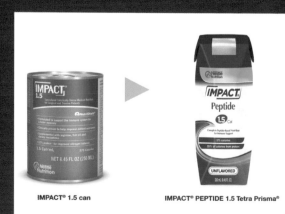

IMPACT® 1.5 can   IMPACT® PEPTIDE 1.5 Tetra Prisma®

Always Innovating

FROM 2011–2012, NESTLÉ HEALTH SCIENCE MADE SIGNIFICANT upgrades in its industrial footprint in North America by adding new technologies, which is expected to have a ripple effect throughout the sector in terms of improvements, said Anna Mohl.

"Overall, it's been a successful endeavor because, while it was a big change in the marketplace, we've really been able to use it to position ourselves in terms of state-of-the-art packaging."

For instance, the company was able to transition its liquid medical nutrition products from cans to Tetra Pak® packaging, as shown in the example to the left. "So you don't have dented cans, which was always a big complaint for our customers, particularly at home. The weight of each case was lighter, and the configuration was smaller. So from a carbon footprint, from a shipping standpoint, and from an ease-of-use standpoint, we could provide big benefits for our customers. It was received very positively and has certainly been part of our selling story, of how we're leading the way in terms of investments in the business, in the category, and in innovation. It's been very successful."

Safe and Effective Weight Loss

While products like *Carnation Breakfast Essentials* and *BOOST* keep Nestlé Health Science in the public eye, other brands make certain that health care professionals always have Nestlé Health Science at the top of their minds.

For many years, when people considered weight loss, they pictured themselves sitting in front of a cup of cottage cheese and an apple—but OPTIFAST® changed all of that when it came into existence over 40 years ago. The brand became part of the Nestlé Health Science portfolio with the acquisition of Novartis Medical Nutrition in 2007.

"*OPTIFAST* really pioneered medical weight management," said Maureen Monahan, head of US sales for the *OPTIFAST* brand line. Patients with obesity who seek to lose a significant amount of weight (typically around 50 pounds) are good candidates for the OPTIFAST program, which combines meal replacement products with behavioral and exercise intervention under the guidance of a doctor and a multi-dimensional team of health care professionals. An individual typically consumes 800 to 960 calories a day for the first 26 weeks as they gain new knowledge about exercise and nutrition. This way, "as they go back to eating regular food, they'll have a different skillset to approach that relationship with food again," Monahan said.

The educational and supervisory component of the OPTIFAST program is so important that patients can't simply buy the product in the store—they must receive it from their physician. The typical OPTIFAST patient loses over 50 pounds in 18–24 weeks. Patients not only enjoy their appearance after weight loss, but some have also experienced other benefits through weight loss, including reductions in their blood pressure or blood cholesterol.

"There are three different formats of the foods with about 13 different choices," Monahan says. "They can have shakes, soups, or bars, and the products are all essentially nutritionally the same. Through five to six servings a day of any combination of those items, they will receive all the nutrition they need for that day. The physician will also schedule how often they're eating to minimize the feeling of hunger between meals."

Over 90 publications cite the effectiveness of the OPTIFAST program. "It's the sole source of nutrition for the patient over 12 to 16 weeks, so we take quality very seriously," Monahan said.

Above: The OPTIFAST products, including shakes, are complete meal replacements exclusively for patients participating in a medically monitored OPTIFAST weight management program.

Below: The OPTIFAST program offers patients three types of weight control products: shakes, bars, and soups.

Right: "Peptamen is our star brand for our medical nutrition portfolio," said Barbara McCartney, former vice president of marketing for North America, now regional business head for consumer care. The product, a peptide-based (pre-digested protein) formula providing complete nutrition, is designed for people whose bodies aren't able to process certain nutrients due to gastrointestinal issues.

Below: Alfamino amino acid formulas provide nutrition for infants and children with multiple food allergies and malabsorptive conditions.

Helping Patients

While some of Nestlé Health Science's products are widely recognized by consumers everywhere, others are more common behind the scenes, as is the case with the company's medical nutrition products.

One such item is the Peptamen® Intense tube-feeding formula that the company launched based on a severe medical need in hospitals. "There were a lot of obese patients in the intensive care unit, and there really wasn't a product that was designed to meet their unique nutritional needs—less calories and more protein," said Carol Siegel, head of medical affairs at Nestlé Health Science in the United States. Siegel leads a team of registered dietitians that provide clinical support for the business.

"We put together a summit on obesity in critical care, so we learned what those needs were, brought that back to the organization, and were able to develop this product. Now it is a very important product for Nestlé Health Science."

Similarly, Nestlé Health Science recently launched Alfamino™ (shown at left), a hypoallergenic free amino acid-based infant formula, and a separate pediatric formula called *Alfamino* Junior for kids with cow's milk protein allergy.

Nestlé Health Science medical professionals don't limit their work to the new products. "If there's a reformulation of a product, we are also very involved in that process," Siegel said. "Quality is extremely important. I think what really shapes our decisions is making sure that what we

provide to the patient is the highest of quality and meets their needs. Whatever standards are out there, you can be sure that Nestlé is two to three steps ahead of that, or the bar is three steps higher than that."

Nestlé Health Science has other products to meet specific medical needs, including enteral feeding tubes that work with enteral pumps and allow patients to continue their activities of daily living as they receive uninterrupted nourishment through tube feeding. Vitaflo, one of the Nestlé Health Science companies, has a series of products for patients with inborn errors of metabolism, while Nestlé Health Science–Pamlab has products designed for the nutritional management of patients with depression, cognitive disorders, and diabetic neuropathy. Prometheus is a leading US diagnostic and therapeutic company active in products for gastrointestinal conditions and oncology.

Above: Juan B. Ochoa, MD, FACS, was inspired by the IMPACT brand to join Nestlé Health Science as chief medical officer in North America. He admired the product and saw Nestlé as a company "focused on trying to do something very good and helping human beings."

Left: Nestlé Health Science is dedicated to providing proven nutritional solutions to improve patients' quality of life.

PHOTO COURTESY OF © BOHM-MARRAZZO STUDIOS

A Medical Mission

Nestlé research and innovation is science based. Juan B. Ochoa, MD, FACS, the chief medical officer for Nestlé Health Science in North America, is helping to lead the charge on that front. Dr. Ochoa joined Nestlé Health Science after gaining an admiration for the company's IMPACT® product, which is specifically designed to meet the distinct nutritional requirements of surgical and trauma patients at high risk for infection.

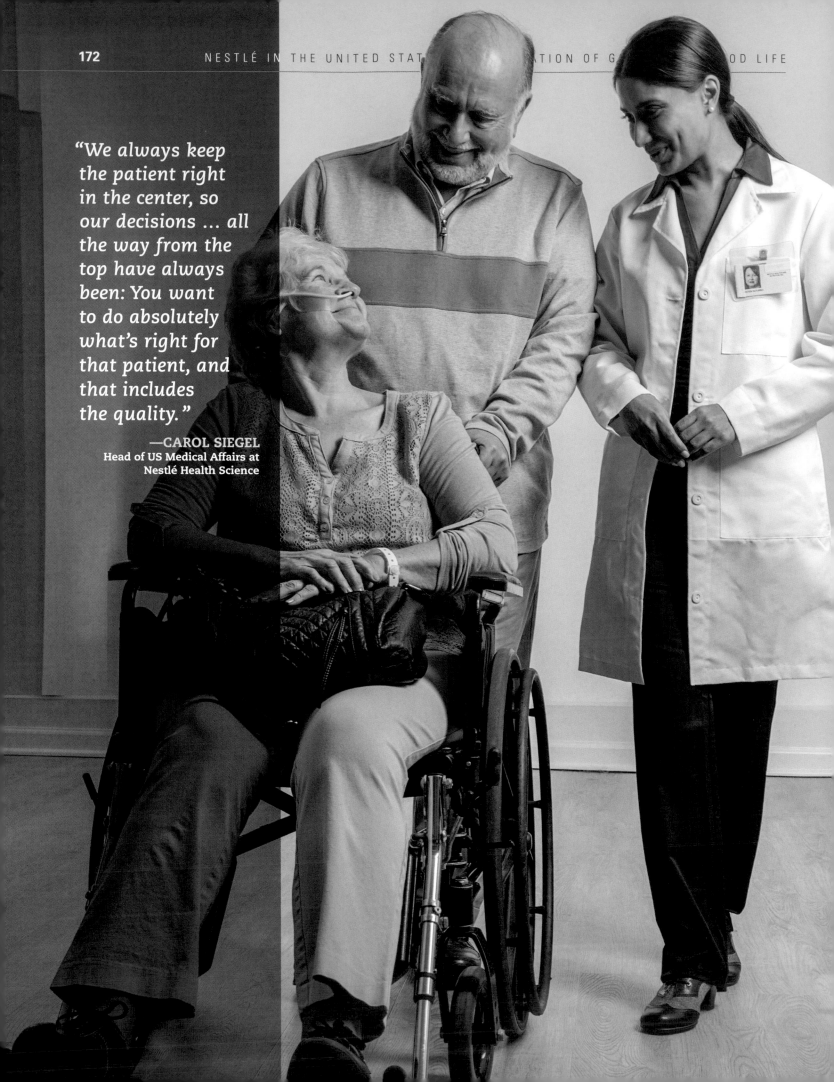

"We always keep the patient right in the center, so our decisions ... all the way from the top have always been: You want to do absolutely what's right for that patient, and that includes the quality."

—CAROL SIEGEL
**Head of US Medical Affairs at
Nestlé Health Science**

"Patients undergoing a major surgical intervention should receive this product before and after surgery as directed by their health care professional," he said. "I have been doing a lot of research for many, many years on the nutrients that are in IMPACT, and it became obvious that it was time for IMPACT to be something these patients should receive." For instance, Nestlé Health Science is currently working on a study of how many protein vs. non-protein calories critically ill patients should receive.

Dr. Ochoa plays several roles at Nestlé Health Science, including educating clinicians about the company's products. His passion for clinical sciences is a key part of his responsibilities. "Our products can indeed demonstrate real patient benefit."

Looking Ahead

Nestlé Health Science has built such momentum in the past decade that there is almost no stopping the sector from charging forward. More innovations will help more consumers receive optimal nutrition.

Nestlé Health Science continues its scientific research to determine how nutrition can be used to help manage diseases and improve health outcomes. Toward that end, the company will open its $70 million Product Technology Center in phases in 2017.

Innovating to improve the quality of care and the health of patients and consumers is the core of Nestlé Health Science. "We work very closely with health care professionals. We get a lot of feedback from them on how our products are working," said Mohl. "We're always looking to understand, from a patient perspective and from a health care professional perspective, what are the needs? Where are the opportunities?"

Above: The Nestlé plant in Anderson, Indiana, produces BOOST nutritional drinks. The factory, which opened in March 2009, also produces Carnation Breakfast Essentials, Coffee-mate, and Nesquik.

Below: Impact Immunonutrition is formulated for patients following major elective surgery or trauma, especially those needing specialized tube feeding and at high risk for infection.

BIBLIOGRAPHY

Books and Articles

Al Ries, "The Dubious Practice of Double Branding," *AdAge*, May 15, 2007.

Anne Cooper Funderburg, *Chocolate, Strawberry, and Vanilla: A History of American Ice Cream*, Bowling Green State University Popular Press, 1995.

Arjun Kharpal, "Nespresso takes a sip of US coffee market," *CNBC*, February 20, 2014.

Bill Berkrot, "Nestlé invests more in skin care strategy with 10 research centers," *Reuters*, December 10, 2014.

Bill Sing, "FTC Approves Nestlé Purchase of Carnation," *Los Angeles Times*, January 5, 1985.

Brandon Griggs, "Oprah picks her 'favorite things' for 2015," *CNN*, November 5, 2015.

Clair Suddath, "Coke Confronts Its Big Fat Problem," *Bloomberg*, July 31, 2014.

Corinne Gretler, "Nestlé Adds Nespresso Factory as U.S. Growth Exceeds Europe," *Bloomberg Business*, September 11, 2015.

Creating Shared Value 2015, copyright Nestlé in the United States.

"De Benedetti Is Selling Buitoni Pasta to Nestlé," *The New York Times*, March 19, 1988.

Dede Wilson, "How Toll House recipe became a cookie-jar staple," *Boston Globe*, April 22, 2014.

Deirdre Pirro, "Giovanni Buitoni: Pasta and chocolate," *The Florentine*, June 16, 2011.

Francesca Donner, "Nespresso's Single-Serve Plan Focuses on China, U.S.," *The Wall Street Journal*, May 21, 2013.

Henri Nestlé: From Pharmacist's Assistant to Founder of the World's Leading Nutrition, Health and Wellness Company, abridged translation by Nestlé for Henri Nestlé's 200th birthday, copyright 1995, Nestlé, p. 67.

James Marshall, *Elbridge A. Stuart, Founder of the Carnation Company*, American Book–Stratford Press, 1949.

Jeff Wells, "The Day Baby Ruths Rained Down on Pittsburgh," *Mental Floss*, October 19, 2015.

Jesus Sanchez, "Nestlé's New Accent: Food: The company will consolidate its U.S. operations under a new leader, the former Carnation president. The idea is to compete better with the giants," *Los Angeles Times*, December 31, 1990.

Joe Weller, *A Blueprint for Success*, 2005.

John D. Weaver, *Carnation: The First 75 Years*, Carnation Company, 1974.

Jon Michaud, "Sweet Morsels: A Sweet History of the Chocolate Chip Cookie," *The New Yorker*, December 19, 2013.

Laura Board, "Nestlé Plumps Up Skin Health with Valeant Deal," *TheStreet*, May 28, 2014.

Leah Zeldes, "Named for slugger or president's kid, candy is Chicago's baby," *Dining Chicago*, June 27, 2011.

Lisa Brown, "Purina adding $15 million office building at downtown campus," *St. Louis Post-Dispatch*, July 15, 2010.

Margot Sanger-Katz, "The Decline of 'Big Soda,'" *The New York Times*, October 2, 2015.

Michael Capuzzo, "Alpo's World of Canine Cuisine Pet-food Makers Say Theirs Is A Dog-eat-dog Business," *Philadelphia Inquirer*, October 19, 1986.

Mike Esterl, "Soft Drinks Hit 10th Year of Decline," *The Wall Street Journal*, March 26, 2015.

Monica Watrous, "Q&A: Nestlé USA putting a fresh spin on frozen," *Food Business News*, July 24, 2015.

"Nestlé Acquires Hills Brothers," *The New York Times*, January 15, 1985.

"Nestlé and Dreyers to Merge in $2.4 Billion Deal, Creating Top U.S. Ice Cream Seller," *The New York Times*, June 18, 2002.

"Nestlé Holdings said it acquired MJB," *Los Angeles Times*, May 10, 1985.

"Nestlé Launches SHIELD Against Impacts of Age, Urbanization," *GCI Magazine*, July 21, 2015.

"Nestlé takes world ice cream lead," *BBC News*, updated January 19, 2006.

"Nestlé USA Commits to Removing Artificial Flavors and FDA-Certified Colors from All Nestlé Chocolate Candy by the End of 2015," press release, *Business Wire*, February 17, 2015.

Pamela G. Hollie, "Carnation: A Family Company's Evolution," *The New York Times*, September 5, 1984.

"Panic of 1893," *Saylor Academy Textbook*, copyright 2015.

Phyllis Hanes, "US chefs compete in international culinary Olympics," *The Christian Science Monitor*, September 11, 1980.

Rachel McDaniel, *Images of America: Pike County*, Arcadia Publishing, 2011.

"Ralston Purina Company," *Encyclopedia Britannica*, updated February 25, 2016.

"RJR Nabisco, Inc. Is Selling Its Baby Ruth, Butterfinger and Pearson Confection Businesses to Nestlé Foods Corp.," *Chicago Tribune*, October 28, 1989.

Robert B. Garlough, *Modern Food Service Purchasing: Business Essentials to Procurement*, Delmar Cengage Learning, p. 73–74.

Roger Mezger, "Nestlé adding Solon product development center," *Cleveland.com*, November 17, 2008.

Salvatore J. LaGumina, Frank J. Cavaioli, Salvatore Primeggia, Joseph A. Varacalli, editors, *The Italian American Experience: An Encyclopedia,* Routledge, 2003.

Sherri Day, "Nestlé and Dreyer's to Merge in $2.4 Billion Deal, Creating Top U.S. Ice Cream Seller," *The New York Times*, Business Day, June 18, 2002.

"Transcript: William H. Danforth, 2007," Washington University School of Medicine Oral History Project, April 24, 2007.

"U.S. Beverage Business Results for 2014," *Beverage-Digest*, Special Issue, March 26, 2015, Vol. 66, No. 7.

Corporate Documents

"About Health and Environment," Nestlé USA internal company document, December 7, 2015.

"About the Nestlé Cocoa Plan," Nestlé USA internal company document, December 17, 2015.

"A Company of Pet Lovers," Nestlé Purina, copyright 2015.

"All about Iced Tea," Nestlé, June 10, 2011.

Arrowhead Bottled Water Quality Report, 2014.

"Carnation Instant Breakfast changes its brand name to Carnation Breakfast Essentials," March 1, 2009.

"Celebrating 75 years of the Nestlé brand that invented instant coffee," Nestlé USA, March 28, 2013.

"Cleveland Food Ingredient Firm Wins Top Honors at 1984 'World Culinary Olympics,'" L. J. Minor Corp. company press release, undated.

Deer Park Bottled Water Quality Report, 2014.

"Discover Casa Buitoni in Tuscany With a Trip for Two to Italy," Buitoni North America press release, October 7, 2010.

"Fueling Sustainability at our Atlanta Plant," Nestlé Purina, November 11, 2013.

"Galderma Laboratories, L.P. Appoints Miles Harrison as Leader of U.S. and Canada," Galderma Press Release, January 11, 2016.

"Gerber Introduces Breakthrough Innovation with New 3rd Foods Lil' Bits Recipes," Gerber press release, April 30, 2015.

"Gerber's history & heritage," Gerber, copyright 2015.

Jack's Pizza, HeritageWerks internal company document, October 14, 2015.

"Meet the famous Gerber Baby," Gerber, copyright 2015.

"Meet the Woman Behind the Culinary Culture at Purina," Nestlé Purina, January 24, 2014.

Minor's Brand Folder, Minor's, copyright 2016.

"Nespresso Expands the VertuoLine Range with the New Evoluo Machine," Nespresso press release, October 1, 2015.

"Nespresso Launches its 2020 Sustainability Ambition, The Positive Cup, and the Nespresso Sustainable Development Fund," Nespresso press release, August 27, 2014.

"Nespresso sets to revolutionise North American Coffee Market," Nespresso, copyright 2016.

"Nestlé Anderson Fact Sheet," Nestlé USA internal company document, November 18, 2015.

Nestlé Confections & Snacks, Nestlé USA, copyright 2016.

"Nestlé deepens commitment to Mexico with Purina Pet Park and factory," Nestlé USA press release, July 11, 2014.

"Nestlé enters global super-premium chocolate category with Swiss chocolate Cailler," Nestlé USA, September 30, 2015.

Nestlé Health Science Introduces Innovative BOOST® Nutritional Drinks in Compact Sizes, Nestlé Health Science press release, July 16, 2015.

"Nestlé Health Science to Invest USD 70 million in Product Technology Center in the U.S.,

dedicated to nutritional therapy innovation," Nestlé Health Science press release, October 9, 2015.

"Nestlé in Ohio," Nestlé USA internal company document.

"Nestlé Launches First Ever Super Bowl Commercial," Nestlé USA, March 3, 2014.

"Nestlé Launches Global R&D Center in Ohio to Address Diverse Consumer Food Demands," Nestlé USA press release, July 22, 2015.

"Nestlé Professional Celebrates the Contributions of Dr. L. J. Minor by Announcing American Culinary Federation's Newly Renamed Dr. L. J. Minor Chef Professionalism Award," Nestlé Professional press release, May 15, 2013.

Nestlé Professional, our company, internal company document.

"Nestlé Purina's Monday Morning Message," Nestlé Purina, copyright 2014.

Nestlé Purina PetCare 2014 Annual Report, Nestlé Purina, August 12, 2015, page 21.

"Nestlé Purina PetCare Honored As One of the Best Places to Work in 2016, A Glassdoor Employees' Choice Award," Nestlé Purina press release, December 9, 2015.

"Nestlé Skin Health partnership to address growing skin health needs," Nestlé press release, December 11, 2014.

"Nestlé Skin Health to Open Global Network of Innovation Hubs to Advance Next Generation of Skin Health," Nestlé press release, December 11, 2014.

Nestlé: The Minor's Story, internal company document.

"Nestlé USA Acquires Fifty Percent Ownership Stake in Ice Cream Partners USA from General Mills," Nestlé press release, December 26, 2001.

Nestlé USA Brand History Report, Beverage, HeritageWerks internal company document, November 6, 2015.

Nestlé USA Brand History Report, Baking, HeritageWerks internal company document, October 14, 2015.

Nestlé USA Brand History Report, Chocolate, HeritageWerks internal company document, October 14, 2015.

Nestlé USA Brand History Report, Coffee, HeritageWerks internal company document, October 14, 2015.

Nestlé USA Brand History Report, Food, HeritageWerks internal company document, November 6, 2015.

Nestlé USA Brand History Report, Ice Cream, HeritageWerks internal company document, November 6, 2015.

Nestlé USA Brand History Report, Sugar, HeritageWerks internal company document, October 14, 2015.

Nestlé USA Corporate Timeline, HeritageWerks internal company document.

Nestlé USA, International Brands Division, Nestlé USA internal company document.

"Nestlé Waters in Pennsylvania," Nestlé Waters North America, copyright 2014.

"Nestlé Waters North America Announces Support For Partnership For A Healthier America's New Drink Up Initiative; First-of-its-kind initiative aimed at encouraging people to drink more water more often," Nestlé press release, September 12, 2013.

Nestlé Waters North America At A Glance, Nestlé Waters North America, copyright 2014.

Nestlé Waters North America At A Glance, Nestlé Waters North America, copyright 2015.

"Nestlé Waters North America Continues Commitment to Wetlands Conservation; #1 Bottled Water Company in the U.S. Contributes $250,000 to Ducks Unlimited,"

Nestlé Waters North America press release, July 26, 2011.

"New *Nespresso* system aims to reshape North American coffee industry," Nestlé press release, April 15, 2016.

"No Arts [Artificial] announcement summary," Nestlé USA internal company report, January 25, 2016.

Official Opening Nestlé Professional Customer Innovation Campus, Nestlé Professional PowerPoint, November 2008.

"Original Nestlé Nesquik Products Take Sweet Steps Towards Better Nutrition," Nestlé USA press release, April 13, 2015.

"Our Partners," Nestlé USA internal company document, December 17, 2015.

"Our Story: 1894–2015, A History of Nestlé Purina PetCare Company in the U.S.," Nestlé Purina, copyright 2015.

"Our Values: The Five Talls," Nestlé Purina, November 2014.

Poland Springs Bottled Water Quality Report, 2014.

"Quality That Goes Beyond the Cup," Nestlé, copyright 2015.

"Ralston Purina Acquisition," Nestlé, copyright 2015.

The Gerber Foundation: History, The Gerber Foundation, copyright 2015.

"The Nespresso History: From A Simple Idea to A Unique Brand Experience," Nespresso, April 2015.

"There's a Holiday for Everything! National Chocolate Covered Raisin Day March 24, 2012," Nestlé USA press release, March 19, 2012.

"What is the nature of Nestlé's relationship with L'Oréal?," Nestlé, copyright 2016.

"When It Comes to Taste, Crema Matters," Nespresso, copyright 2016.

Zephyrhills Bottled Water Quality Report, 2014.

Internet Research

"A Taste of Libby's Pumpkin History," Nestlé website, accessed December 11, 2015.

"Better Buildings Are Our Legacy," United States Green Building Council website, accessed December 21, 2016.

"Creator of the Chocolate Chip Cookie," All About Chocolate Chip Cookies website, accessed May 23, 2016.

Crystal Springs Foundation website, about us, accessed December 14, 2015.

Crystal Springs Foundation website, founders, accessed December 14, 2015.

DiGiorno website, our story, accessed November 25, 2015.

"Dreyer's Grand Ice Cream Oral History Project," University of California–Berkeley Library website, accessed December 1, 2015.

"Flavor Is The One Thing That Will Bring Customers Back Again And Again," Minor's website, accessed January 7, 2016.

"Frozen Pizza Facts," National Frozen Pizza Institute website, accessed May 23, 2016.

"Frozen pizza: Market Statistics & Industry Facts," Statista website, accessed May 23, 2016.

Galderma website, company history, accessed December 14, 2015.

Gerber Life Insurance Company website, Child Life Insurance, accessed February 24, 2016.

Häagen-Dazs website, our history, accessed December 1, 2015.

"Henri Nestlé," Nestlé website, accessed May 23, 2016.

"Hiding in Plain Sight," Vanishing St. Louis website, accessed January 8, 2016.

Leadership in Energy and Environmental Design (LEED), Nestlé Waters North America website, accessed December 7, 2015.

"Libby's History," corporate video, accessed December 11, 2015.

Mintz, S., & McNeil, S. (2016). "The Depression of the Mid-1890s." *Digital History*. Retrieved May 23, 2016 from http://www.digitalhistory.uh.edu/disp_textbook.cfm?smtID=2&psid=3125.

Nescafé website, coffee mythbusting, accessed May 23, 2016.

Nespresso website, partners, accessed May 23, 2016.

"Nestlé Chocolate Bar History," The Old Time Candy Company website, accessed May 23, 2016.

Nestlé Crunch website, about, accessed May 23, 2016.

Nestlé Nesquik website, our story, accessed May 23, 2016.

"Oh Henry!," Nestlé USA website, accessed May 23, 2016.

"Our History: Milk Based Food," Nestlé website, accessed May 23, 2016.

Ovaltine UK website, about us, accessed May 23, 2016.

Ozarka Waters website, our story, accessed February 1, 2016.

"Perrier," Nestlé Waters North America website, accessed January 18, 2016.

Peter Superlative Chocolate website, history, accessed May 23, 2016.

"Poland Spring: Summering in Fashion," Maine Historical Society website, accessed December 22, 2015.

"Promoting Self-sufficiency Through Community Education and Development," Merage Family Foundation website, accessed November 25, 2015.

"Ralston Purina Company," encyclopedia.com website, accessed February 1, 2016.

"Rock House Cave Preservation," Eureka Springs Parks and Recreation Commission website, accessed December 10, 2015.

"Stouffer Corp. History," Funding Universe website, accessed December 13, 2015.

"Stouffer Corporation," Ohio History Connection website, accessed December 1, 2015.

"Stouffer Foods," The Encyclopedia of Cleveland History website, accessed December 1, 2015.

"Stuart Family," *Forbes* website, accessed January 7, 2016.

Stuart Foundation website, history, accessed January 7, 2016.

"The Minor's Story," Minor's website, accessed November 10, 2015.

Nestlé website, company history, accessed October 14, 2015.

Nestlé website, our brands, accessed October 14, 2015.

Tombstone Pizza website, our story, accessed November 25, 2015.

"Water Quality," Acqua Panna website, accessed April 15, 2016.

"William H. Danforth Ralston Purina, Danforth Foundation," University of Missouri–St. Louis website, accessed February 1, 2016.

"Wonka," Nestlé website, accessed May 23, 2016.

Interviews

Bill Biggar, interview by Jeffrey L. Rodengen, digital recording, 10 December 2015, Write Stuff Enterprises, LLC.

Jim Biggar, interview by Jeffrey L. Rodengen, digital recording, 10 December 2015, Write Stuff Enterprises, LLC.

Tim Brown, interview by Jeffrey L. Rodengen, digital recording, 10 November 2015, Write Stuff Enterprises, LLC.

John Carmichael, interview by Jeffrey L. Rodengen, digital recording, 10 December 2015, Write Stuff Enterprises, LLC.

Judy Cascapera, interview by Jeffrey L. Rodengen, digital recording, 15 December 2015, Write Stuff Enterprises, LLC.

Rob Case, interview by Jeffrey L. Rodengen, digital recording, 28 December 2015, Write Stuff Enterprises, LLC.

Louise DeFalco, interview by Jeffrey L. Rodengen, digital recording, 18 December 2015, Write Stuff Enterprises, LLC.

Molly Dell'Omo, interview by Jeffrey L. Rodengen, digital recording, 26 October 2015, Write Stuff Enterprises, LLC.

Susanna Forteleoni, interview by Jeffrey L. Rodengen, digital recording, 15 December 2015, Write Stuff Enterprises, LLC.

Paul Grimwood, interview by Jeffrey L. Rodengen, digital recording, 26 October 2015, Write Stuff Enterprises, LLC.

Jeff Hamilton, interview by Jeffrey L. Rodengen, digital recording, 10 December 2015, Write Stuff Enterprises, LLC.

Laura Hardin, interview by Jeffrey L. Rodengen, digital recording, 22 October 2015, Write Stuff Enterprises, LLC.

Kim Jeffery, interview by Jeffrey L. Rodengen, digital recording, 10 November 2015, Write Stuff Enterprises, LLC.

Katerina Kakanas, interview by Jeffrey L. Rodengen, digital recording, 11 December 2015, Write Stuff Enterprises, LLC.

Robert Kilmer, interview by Jeffrey L. Rodengen, digital recording, 5 January 2016, Write Stuff Enterprises, LLC.

Bob Kosters, interview by Jeffrey L. Rodengen, digital recording, 25 October 2015, Write Stuff Enterprises, LLC.

Jane Lazgin, interview by Jeffrey L. Rodengen, digital recording, 30 November 2015, Write Stuff Enterprises, LLC.

Nina Leigh, interview by Jeffrey L. Rodengen, digital recording, 15 December 2015, Write Stuff Enterprises, LLC.

Barbara McCartney, interview by Jeffrey L. Rodengen, digital recording, 16 November 2015, Write Stuff Enterprises, LLC.

Patrick W. McGinnis, interview by Jeffrey L. Rodengen, digital recording, 8 December 2015, Write Stuff Enterprises, LLC.

Perry Miele, interview by Jeffrey L. Rodengen, digital recording, 15 October 2015, Write Stuff Enterprises, LLC.

Anna Mohl, interview by Jeffrey L. Rodengen, digital recording, 30 November 2015, Write Stuff Enterprises, LLC.

Maureen Monahan, interview by Jeffrey L. Rodengen, digital recording, 16 November 2015, Write Stuff Enterprises, LLC.

Andrew Muniak, interview by Jeffrey L. Rodengen, digital recording, 15 December 2015, Write Stuff Enterprises, LLC.

Virginie Naigeon, interview by Jeffrey L. Rodengen, digital recording, 4 February 2016, Write Stuff Enterprises, LLC.

Juan Ochoa, interview by Jeffrey L. Rodengen, digital recording, 23 November 2015, Write Stuff Enterprises, LLC.

Roz O'Hearn, interview by Jeffrey L. Rodengen, digital recording, 10 December 2015, Write Stuff Enterprises, LLC.

Bill Partyka, interview by Cathy Dunn, 15 June 2016, e-mailed to Jeffrey L. Rodengen, Write Stuff Enterprises, LLC.

James Pergola, interview by Jeffrey L. Rodengen, digital recording, 11 December 2015, Write Stuff Enterprises, LLC.

Hyder Raheem, interview by Jeffrey L. Rodengen, digital recording, 10 December 2015, Write Stuff Enterprises, LLC.

Keith M. Schopp, interview by Jeffrey L. Rodengen, digital recording, 7 December 2015, Write Stuff Enterprises, LLC.

Carol Siegel, interview by Jeffrey L. Rodengen, digital recording, 16 November 2015, Write Stuff Enterprises, LLC.

Joe Sivewright, interview by Jeffrey L. Rodengen, digital recording, 7 December 2015, Write Stuff Enterprises, LLC.

Tom Smith, interview by Jeffrey L. Rodengen,
    digital recording, 26 October 2015,
    Write Stuff Enterprises, LLC.
Eric Somnolet, interview by Jeffrey L. Rodengen,
    digital recording, 16 November 2015,
    Write Stuff Enterprises, LLC.
Cam Starrett, interview by Jeffrey L. Rodengen,
    digital recording, 4 December 2015,
    Write Stuff Enterprises, LLC.
Aileen Stocks, interview by Jeffrey L. Rodengen,
    digital recording, 16 November 2015,
    Write Stuff Enterprises, LLC.
Carol Stropki, interview by Jeffrey L. Rodengen,
    digital recording, 15 October 2015,
    Write Stuff Enterprises, LLC.
Patrick Todd, interview by Jeffrey L. Rodengen,
    digital recording, 16 November 2015,
    Write Stuff Enterprises, LLC.
Carlos Velasco, interview by Jeffrey L. Rodengen,
    digital recording, 17 December 2015,
    Write Stuff Enterprises, LLC.
John Vella, interview by Jeffrey L. Rodengen,
    digital recording, 8 December 2015,
    Write Stuff Enterprises, LLC.

Joe Weller, interview by Jeffrey L. Rodengen,
    digital recording, 30 November 2015,
    Write Stuff Enterprises, LLC.
Robyn Wimberly, interview by Jeffrey
    L. Rodengen, digital recording, 16 November
    2015, Write Stuff Enterprises, LLC.

Newsletters

Nestlé's News, September 1955, published by
    The Nestlé Company, Inc., White Plains,
    New York.
Nestlé's News, December 1955, published by
    The Nestlé Company, Inc., White Plains,
    New York.
Nestlé's News, March 1956, published by
    The Nestlé Company, Inc., White Plains,
    New York.
Nestlé's News, June 1956, published by
    The Nestlé Company, Inc., White Plains,
    New York.
Nestlé's News, December 1957, published by
    The Nestlé Company, Inc., White Plains,
    New York.

INDEX

Nestlé 150 Years

of Good Food, Good Life

1977

Thanks in part to the efforts of L. J. Minor Corp., the US Department of Labor, and the American Culinary Federation announce that the role of executive chef is moving from the "services" category to the "professional, technical, and managerial occupations" category in the *Dictionary of Official Titles.*

1982

Fancy Feast®, the first-ever gourmet cat food in single-serve cans, is launched.

1985

Nestlé buys Carnation Company. At the time, the $3 billion deal makes headlines as it is the largest non-oil acquisition in history.

Carnation

L. J. Minor Corp. joins Nestlé, bringing with it a portfolio of hundreds of products that make a chef's day easier.

1987

Purina debuts super-premium lines of dog food, including Pro Plan® and Purina® ONE®.

1990

Nestlé acquires Baby Ruth® and Butterfinger® from RJR Nabisco. Bart Simpson becomes Butterfinger's spokesman, threatening, "Nobody better lay a finger on my Butterfinger®."

1994

SKINNY COW® brand ice cream snacks debut.

1998

Nestlé inaugurates a new research and development facility in Princeton, New Jersey.

200

Nest
purch
comp
whic
half
bottl
busi
it int
billio
Nest

A Timeline of Key Events in the History

1981

Nestlé & L'Oréal form a joint venture solely dedicated to dermatology called Galderma.

GALDERMA

Lean Cuisine® debuts with 10 products—a culmination of testing begun 14 years earlier.

1983

The single-serving, handheld frozen convenience food Hot Pockets® hits the market.

1986

Nespresso® is founded. Inspired by Luiggi Bezzera's original espresso coffee concept, the company develops a revolutionary system of portioned, encapsulated coffee, and dedicated machines to deliver perfect coffee.

1988

Nestlé purchases Buitoni® for $1.27 billion. In the US, Buitoni joins the Carnation division.

Nestlé launches its infant formula line in the United States under the name Carnation® Good Start®.

Nestlé buys the Willy Wonka® candy brand.

1992

Nestlé acquires Perrier Group of America and renames the business Nestlé Waters.

1996

DiGiorno® pizza comes on the market. It is the first frozen pizza to introduce a rising crust.

1999

Nestlé begins a joint venture with Häagen-Dazs®, and the brand, which has grown to include gelato, frozen yogurt, and ice cream bars, was officially licensed to Nestlé in 2001.

Two other imported brands join the Nestlé Waters family: Acqua Panna®, an Italian still water that traces its roots back centuries, and S.Pellegrino®, an Italian sparkling water.

200

Nest
Ralst
move
care
as pa
creat
PetCa

Gerb
first c
Unite
produ
asept
(vege